Gutted

Gutted

How An Old House Remodeled Me

MAIDA KORTE

SHE WRITES PRESS

Published in 2026 by
She Writes Press, an imprint of The Stable Book Group

1569 Solano Ave #546
Berkeley, CA 94707
https://shewritespress.com
Library of Congress Control Number: 2026904416
ISBN: 979-8-89636-336-1
eISBN: 979-8-89636-337-8

Interior Designer: Tabitha Lahr

Printed in the United States

This book is memoir. It reflects the author's present recollections of experiences over time. Names and identifying characteristics have been changed to protect the privacy of certain individuals.

To Kimberly, Kerianne, Heather, and Miranda, who together form my launch and my landing.

And of course, to Andy, who will only know this book by my reading it to him as we drive far, far away and always return to the same place. Here.

Preface

Whether we are transient in our natural habitat of hearth and home, or have deep roots anchoring generations of family in one geographical location, we all claim some "place" to be ours alone. Although my own personal experiences of dwelling places have never taken me very far away from where I started, the often subtle and sometimes dramatic changes from one place to the next have all loomed large to me.

Perhaps that is why I chose design as my professional calling. Discovering how someone wants to live and work is, to me, an archaeological dig into the inner workings of a person, a family, a home, a heritage. I help people see space in a new way, with the hope that this will enhance their lives. The odyssey is sometimes obvious and deliberate, and other times nuanced and subtle, craft measured with illumination, not forgetting the important tidbit of surprise. Though mastering this art for others and helping countless people change their lives by moving from one space to another is something I enjoy doing and am skilled at, doing it for myself and my family has been another experience entirely.

I had lived in the city of Chicago nearly all my life when my husband, Andy, carried me off to the country to live right on the edge of where rural meets drop-off. With four daughters in tow, and a life filled with drama and hair accessories, we set forth with our proverbial covered wagon and discovered along the way that a new life in an old house had challenges we could not have imagined.

While the spark of inspiration in design may come from the smallest of things, such as a lamp picked up at a garage sale or the desire to create a little niche off the kitchen to dine together as a family, our inspiration for moving to the country was a foggy notion that a big old house would be fun. I know, I know, I know. I would have made lists in chart form for any client's request. A design project would have been tackled by first making rational decisions with detailed renovation plans and budget numbers attached to each item. I would have explored, with teams of experts, the fundamental and mechanical elements of the home, and I would have measured all the dreams against the practical realities. We did none of this and just jumped. Right in.

The complications of making an old house behave and take responsibility for itself is like training a large but kindly beast to lean forward—ever so nicely, please—and touch its toes. It can't, and it won't. What was equally surprising was what we saw in ourselves throughout the journey. All the trials of quick-drying cement drying too quickly, windows that would not open, sinkholes to China, and bats circling our heads in the attic led us to see that our childlike notions of wonder could expand. We brought shenanigans into our lives just when we thought they might be lost forever.

My remodeling work had renewed countless spaces for my clients, through which I learned to navigate tears, frustration, and even temper tantrums in others, but the screw that held my emotions in check loosened when I was working on my own space. With every wall torn down and every new cabinet installed, emotions ran high.

What started as a quest to lift an old house out of its misery turned into an unexpected look at where life had taken me and where I was headed. I saw that the tightfisted hold responsibility had on my heart needed to be unwound, finger by finger, one knuckle at a time. Like a neglected house being opened to fresh air and light, this move from the city to the country allowed my soul to be penetrated by a renewed wisdom and the whisper of a simpler life.

Beginnings

*Once the tugboat takes you out to the ocean liner,
you got to get all the way on board. Can't straddle
both decks.*
> —Katherine Paterson, *The Great Gilly Hopkins*

The day we came to see the house that would become our
home, it was a hot summer Sunday afternoon in July
2004. The sky was so intensely blue that it hurt my eyes. As
I pulled the visor down to shield myself from the throbbing
sunlight, we exited the expressway with thirty miles to go.
The two-lane road we traveled through a countryside lined
with wooden fences and blank-faced cows was enough of
a difference from the pulse of an energetic city life for me
to feel an anxiety talon creeping into my initial excitement.

We were considering moving away from the city, where
all four of my daughters had been born and raised, our
female souls tethered to thick traffic, streetlights, and tight
neighborhoods. We stood on a precipice, facing a decision
we knew would change our lives. Would we jump or reel

backwards, back to the city we knew, or did my husband's innocent desire bear consideration? This moment originated from a simple moment of his compulsion.

"Will we never live somewhere different?" Andy asked one evening. I bridled at this startling question. My husband is a quiet man, unobtrusive, an uncomplaining soul. He rarely registers dissatisfaction, and I wondered how long he had been thinking about this.

"What? Where?"

His gentle suggestion that we could perhaps move to Montana prompted me to answer that I would cry every day. I imagined a lonely existence that would require manual labor, something I am not averse to, having hauled debris out of multiple remodeling projects, but I did worry about the unknown aspect of how we would carve out a life for ourselves in the vacant West.

"Why do you want to move away from our life?" A slight tremor in my voice as I asked the question pestered me. "Is this a new revelation for you? How long have you wanted to move?"

"As long as I can remember. I hate living in the city, always have."

I was stunned by Andy's response. We had fallen in love in the city where he lived when I met him, we had married in the city, and lived with my daughters in a small house in the city. It never occurred to me that he held such a fervent and negative opinion of Chicago. This new and disturbing fact drove me to solve this problem, forgetting that I loved city life, and shoving the truth about my own urban personality into a mental suitcase and slamming it shut. I could not bear, though, the isolation that would come from moving out West. Also, I could not imagine my girls having the lives they dreamed of with such a drastic eruption of lifestyle.

With our marriage, a second one for both of us, Andy had embraced my life of girls times four, and I felt it was only fair that I tamp down my city dreams and embrace his. Abandoning the Montana suggestion, our compromise was to look northwest, to the rural outskirts of Chicago.

On this sunshine day, we had been followed to Woodstock, a small town seventy miles northwest of Chicago, by friends from the city who could not believe we were considering moving so far away.

"You are going to the edge of the world!" cried Maria, my cohort in child-rearing. Her husband Kurt trailed behind us as Maria moaned her protest.

I met Maria when we were both newlyweds and did not have a scratch nickel between us. We made important decisions, like having a baby, the way we made most of our decisions at that time: with minimal consideration.

"I think I'm pregnant." I spoke these words as we sat together sipping coffee. I had a murky realization that my life was about to change.

"Cool!"

"We can push strollers together," I offered.

"Cool! Kurt?"

"Huh? Uh, OK." This response from Maria's husband spoke volumes about our innocent attitude toward parenting.

We soon found ourselves raising nine children between us. The bond that comes from being young and not realizing that you are quite poor, while at the same time being idealistic, runs deep and wide. We gather a sense of ownership to the friendships that erupt from early, shared life experiences. Learning how to raise a family, be a wife, cook meals, fix broken appliances, read bedtime stories, and fold mountains of laundry, all while displaying personal idiosyncrasies that make me cringe in retrospect, was shared with a few women doing the same thing at the same time. We were finding out who we were as women and what we thought about life. We discussed evolution, creationism, classic literature, Greek mythology, new math, hair removal, and chore charts. As we planned home schooling lesson plans to be shared among our children, we were putting down deep roots of friendship, anchoring us to the city. We could walk everywhere we needed to go, and neighborhoods were tight and small, making them easy to navigate with clutching children and wobbly strollers. The energy of city life blended well with our nearly electric grab at life each day. We were busy, filled with energy and ideas. Sidewalks gave paths to our days and streetlights pointed us toward each other at night.

But now, it was unimaginable that I could give this up for pastures, fields of corn, and cows. Maria's reaction to my casual remark about going to look at a house far from our stroller-rutted Chicago scape did not surprise me. She would follow me, of course, so that she could talk me out of this inane idea.

Before I could catch a wisp of country air, and before the actual decision to move was made, I didn't know that I was about to fall in love with a house.

As we drove into what would be our new old town for the very first time, Maria and Kurt in tow, we navigated our way past little shops in the downtown area, all quaint and welcoming, beckoning me to look around. But Andy was a man on a mission. Locating a hilly road three blocks from the town square, he slowed to a crawl. A large four-square Victorian loomed up, blossom-like before us, and it was so different from anything "Chicago" that we found ourselves laughing out of the innocent shock that comes from audacious surprise.

No high-rises, gangways, or alleys, and rather than a sprinkling of the occasional tree, a lush green lawn rose before us, and shrubbery that I could not name was punctuated with a sprawling magenta magnolia and a maple that towered over the walkway to the front porch, making me feel canopied and my arrival heralded. As we stood and stared at the porch that wrapped its way around the front and side of the house, we could see chairs with comfy cushions and a hanging swing. Before we could speak, a marching band began to play, and we had not even made it to the front door when John Philip Sousa accompanied our own parade up the walk. This crash of cymbals and rat-a-tat drum cadence heard from three blocks away, and the cheers of an unknown crowd, was more than our urban sensibilities could handle, and Maria and I fell into hysterics.

"Settle down," was all Andy said as I attempted to muffle my laughter.

Stoic, ever calm in the face of disaster, the clear opposite of the catalog of emotions I displayed nearly every day. He found me charming and delightful, even though my reactions would have most certainly annoyed anyone else.

Unbeknownst to us, this day was an annual event in Woodstock when they celebrated, with wild regalia, the cult classic film *Groundhog Day*, which was filmed here in 1993. I am certain the "townies," as they proudly liked to be called, did not plan on living life as a movie set, but it seemed no one here could let it go. It was as though they had a town meeting when they saw the movie reviews coming in and decided collectively to redesign their entire community around the "I was there" mentality that major events bring. Signs were posted that bragged: "Bill Murray sat here during the restaurant scene." A beautifully engraved solid bronze plaque, set in sidewalk stone, told us the exact spot where Murray stepped in that puddle.

I bit my lip not only to compose myself from further laughter, but to relish this moment of rural joy that seemed to bubble up all around us unabated. This was not an Iowa sensibility of self-control but rather a Midwestern display of unfettered pride and joy. I could not believe the sheer delight of it all.

Even though a certain excitement was palpable, and I found myself caught up in the wonderment of what I considered to be small-town doings, I did have city-directed misgivings. I was worried that our little Chicago bungalow would feel bad about not having a large, sprawling wraparound porch. It tried so hard and even boasted a little front portico.

Bungalows are famous in Chicago and the varieties are practically endless, but a few elements are common to all. On the exterior, brick is the norm, though ours was balloon frame with a Potemkin façade of wood siding. The house was unique in that it sat in the middle of a wide lot and was less than half a block from the metro. Our well-positioned Chicago bungalow, and the others around it, were built with neat little rows of rooms. Living spaces on one side of the house, bedrooms and bathrooms on the other, kitchen in the back—these are common to all bungalows. A central hall generally leads from the front door to the back kitchen, where a possible porch is the caboose. The hall may be a straight line, or it can meander off the path momentarily, taking a little turn to an interesting built-in cabinet holding a dozen tiny doors and drawers, and then return to doing its job leading people to the back where sunlight can again be found streaming in from the windows on the opposite end. By bringing light into the house in this way, the bungalow is a brilliant design. Narrow gangways of concrete, crushed gravel, or brightly colored brick pavers run between every house, and walking from front sidewalk to back alley means being able to touch the houses on either side with your hands.

The safety of small, tight houses gave boundary to the intense expectations that I faced every day. The condensed hecticness was measurable, and I felt at home with quick decisions and curt, sharp directives. Even before Andy mentioned a desire to move out of the city, I could feel in my bones that slowing down might be on the horizon, and I was scared of the realization that my whole life was about to change. I was not a woman who slowed down. I marched through life with determination and could not let up for a single second—else who knows what might happen? Everything would fall apart, and I might discover that I did not know who I was. Life had never allowed for rest and reflection, and the gears inside my head had on and off buttons with nothing in between. The suggestion that there might be another way to live was clearly an unknown that freaked me out, but at the same time beckoned to me.

Our Chicago home was orderly, as if it were holding itself tight with arms positioned at its sides to conserve space on a crowded bus. Chicago homes must mind their own business and cannot let bedrooms just amble out and away from the central body of the home since there just is not room to do so. When newer city houses want to reach out and peek into the spaces beyond, they must reach up rather than out. Kitchens are separated from living rooms and dining rooms not by archway entrances, but by fourteen stair risers that become narrower and steeper the higher up you go. Designing and remodeling homes has had me visit a prospective client by walking up a flight to say hello, walking up another flight to hang up my coat, and walking down two flights to use the restroom.

As accustomed as I was to urban living, I could not have imagined that I would one day visit an aging grand dame of a house far away from city streets that would captivate me enough to woo me away. I felt neat and orderly in Chicago, and this held my Type A self together. My anxious mind mimicked the combined elements of our house by allowing me to put my emotions into neat little rooms. I would access my feelings and thoughts when necessary, put them away again, and then shut the door gently so as not to wake other occupants.

The minutiae of daily responsibility were camouflaged by fast-paced urban living. When fear rose up inside me, it was well-hidden by the clipped pace my lifestyle and setting afforded me in the city. An entourage of anxiety followed me, and I did not like the long shadow that was becoming my daily companion. I was nearly angry with myself for even pondering the move to the country. Forming a methodology to handle my emotions and keep them in check had taken years. It was hard for me to imagine living a new way.

I had been a nervous little girl, with recollections of worry and dread as far back as I can remember. Anxiety haunted me, and I could not have named it, so I settled into the land of perfection. A good girl, I reveled in the praise of my parents and anyone doling it out. Losing my mother's rattail comb one day at the town swimming pool had me collapsing on the back seat of our station wagon in a puddle of sobs. It is here that my sweet and kind mother found me, not having the slightest idea of why I was so inconsolable.

"I lost your comb! I lost it! I can't find it and I put it in my towel and I lost it, it's gone. It's gone! I lost it, Mommy, I lost it!"

Haltingly, gulping for air, hot tears on a summer day streaming down my face, gasping out the words, I relaxed as my mother wrapped me in her arms, crying herself. She only knew to comfort me in the now, whispering and rocking and telling me that she could buy another comb. My mom didn't know how to name what she saw as an emotional hole needing to be filled, and in her sweet spirit she set out to make life as wonderful as possible for me and my five siblings. For every praise I received, and I received a lot, it cemented my view that by being as perfect as possible, I could hold at bay the monster of worry that lived in the basement of my mind. I was brash enough to venture down there every so often, never understanding why I would seek trouble. The plan for perfection was working, so I set my jaw. I began a counting game in my mind, blending the need for perfection with the calming effect I received from organizing letters and numbers. This mental game seemed to temporarily quiet the jumbled mass of disconnected thoughts.

"Maida, what is your goal for your fourth-grade year?" Mrs. Hamilton had asked this question to each of my classmates and now it was my turn. She had made a lovely chart with each child's name next to rows and columns. I adore charts and neat piles of anything, so I was beyond excited to clearly state, "Straight A's every report card." Mrs. Hamilton gave me a quizzical look, since my classmates had stated things like learning to play the clarinet, or to become a hall monitor, or win the school trophy in basketball. Ultimately, I'm sure she was not surprised as I doggedly pursued this goal, missing out on the free-fall fun of the other kids my age, but since this held anxiety pinned and quiet, I persisted.

As we walked up the stairs and onto the front porch, a realtor opened the entrance door. Andy put his hand on the small of my back, not to guide me but to remind me why we were there.

"For God's sake, stop laughing," Andy whispered into my ear, nudging me forward. Normally Andy didn't mind my overreactions, but he wasn't sure this would be interpreted by the realtor as nervous excitement. Nudging him back, I shot him a look which he ignored, but I did muffle my giggles.

I never expected to love this house and adopted an aloof attitude as I walked through the front door. As we wandered through the small tile-detailed vestibule, there was a fireplace directly across the room in my line of sight. Walking over, I found myself reaching out to touch the ionic columns in quarter-sawn oak that stood on either side. I quickly withdrew my hand. There were converging solid oak pocket doors, two inches thick, on the adjoining wall dividing the rooms. Carved crown moldings edged all the ceilings. Leaded glass graced every exterior door, and character dripped like frosting down the sides of a bundt cake. I had a keen eye for detail after laboring in the field of design for several decades at this point, but I barely knew where to look since every trim molding, every floor pattern held intricacy. The touch of a master craftsman was evident everywhere, and even if some elements appeared worn and tired, I could see the presence of artisans at work over one hundred years ago.

The rooms were large and spacious, and I had an over-whelming desire to spread my arms wide open and spin around to see what it would feel like to spiral slowly with head back, eyes closed, and not touch anything. The intoxication of space began to shift my resolve. Andy looked at me and smiled. He could tell that I was weakening, and so he walked over to me and took my hand.

"Like?"

"Don't talk to me."

Our friends wandered from room to room. We were a mute parade on sensory overload, and the drug was wide-open interior space. The second floor had bedrooms with little transom windows above each door. These little awning windows had slider hinges in solid brass, dulled with age but fully functional. They could be angle-opened at night, allowing gentle breezes into the rooms. I found this mesmerizing and played with the pinch operators at the bottom of each brass rod. There were large old closets, built-in cabinets for linens, stairs to a walk-up attic, and interesting angles and mysteries to be discovered with every door I opened.

I could not help but wonder if a parallel existed between my fascination for this house and the inner work I knew I needed to do. I was not completely blind to the multiple renovation projects this house would require, but I was very good at turning a blind eye to the personal overhauls my emotional self required. The grind of holding my inner demons at bay had me wound tightly. I pondered my need to keep going, rarely resting, ever pressing, pushing forward. I had learned to exist, even cope, and possibly flourish, but my luster and love of life was dimming. This realization was compelling me to build something new that would bring a quietness to my family, since I did not know how to gentle my own spirit.

My parents were young when they died, yet they had twenty-five grandchildren, which still astonishes me even though I lived through and experienced the cadence of birth, birth, birth. As I looked around the walk-up attic with its windowed dormers, crow's nest, and high ceilings, I reflected on how families expand for a flash, a moment in time, and then—*poof!*—they are gone. The years being lived right now, right at this very minute, were filled with the busyness that comes from high school exams, college visits, and sporting events: the ever-present demands of parenting four children growing up too fast. I did not want to miss a single scene this future would bring, so clutching Andy's hand tightly, my head turning right and left to memorize the space, I decided to borrow his confidence. My husband wanted us to be part of a wild and glorious future, filled with the chaos the coming years would bring. Andy was also aware that there would be challenge mixed with joy, but he was unafraid and wanted to hoist me up next to him in the western-bound saddle, and so I relented.

There was a lot wrong with the house, but we did not care on this blue-sky day with a parade in the background. This day was about wraparound porches and walnut trees and intoxicating lilacs visible from nearly every window. Towering long-needle pines reaching fifty feet high lined the back fence. They were catching a slight breeze that moved the tall branches as gentle as a lullaby. This day was about old wine cellars where ice used to be stored for refrigeration, coal chutes with blackened walls, and a crow's nest above the attic that had stairs taking us up and out to see the world from high above the other houses. Beyond the driveway sat a carriage house converted to a garage, where hay was thrown down onto waiting horse buggies a very long time ago. Everywhere I looked I saw a dream forming. A vision of grandbabies visiting and putting on shows for us as they dressed up in costumes from the attic. A dream that included walking on cobblestone streets, pancake breakfasts, pie-eating contests, ice-cream cones, and soda fountains. My mind exploded with the picturesque possibilities.

What we could not (or would not) see on this day were the problems lurking behind the plaster. Exposed electrical wires with cloth fraying over bare electrical current, leaking pipes, faucets that did not work, and cracks in every wall and ceiling. We refused to acknowledge the lack of insulation and the high energy bills that would ensue. Sewer pipes were ready to explode under the front lawn, there was the future discovery of hidden water damage, and oh, did I mention the bats circling unbeknownst to us in the attic? On this day we did not see any of that, and as Sousa's "The Washington Post March" began to play in the distance, we knew we would buy this house.

City Girl

I never saw a purple cow, I never hope to see one; but
I can tell you, anyhow, I'd rather see than be one.
                    —Gelett Burgess, "The Purple Cow"

"Honey, I can't. I just can't." Admitting this to my husband was hard, since we had already seen the house and it had been love at first sight. While Andy was figuring out the necessary steps for moving, I was reliving every city moment that I had experienced over the previous twenty-five years.

Growing up in a western suburb of Chicago, there was always lots of room outdoors. We had a small house built on a slab of concrete, and "the four big kids" slept in one bedroom. Two matching sets of bunk beds lined the walls, and it was here that I learned the only interior space I could call mine, for a very long time, was my upper-bunk twin bed. I placed all my little girl things at the foot of my bed, from dolls to books to trinkets of great importance, like a small red ball and a fur muff given to me by my grandmother. No matter the day's events, I could retreat to this defined space, feeling cloistered and comforted from the din of activity around me.

My sister and brothers and I played outside all the time. From first thing in the morning until the six o'clock whistle sounded, signaling the time to run home for dinner, we played in our consigned and unspoken groups until the shadows of evening fell. Once dinner and any subsequent chores were completed, we raced outdoors again to partake in a different set of evening games: tag in various forms, kick-the-can, just plain chasing each other, or listening to scary stories told by the big kids—until the entire neighborhood somehow knew collectively that it was time to go inside and get ready for bed. One by one, kids disappeared into homes, and stragglers scuffed the ground and eventually followed the trail into window-lit bedrooms of their own.

I remember running all the time. We ran to our neighbors, ran across the street, ran down the block, ran to get the ball, ran away from dogs, ran away from the big boys, ran to explore Billy Goat's Gruff, ran to tell my brothers at the baseball diamond to come home—running without ever being tired. Tiring was being called home to do chores, like washing the inside of the car while my brothers sprayed the exterior with a hose, smearing the dirt into circular patterns with rags. Tiring was walking to school or cleaning my room or having to stop jumping rope. I recall being wide awake all the time, until the protests dimmed and eyelids fluttered, and then sleep came in a sudden slam, never the gentle whisper of slumber.

Dogs also ran everywhere in my early childhood neigh-borhood. Often right beside us, roaming free, never on a leash; we would have scoffed at the thought of it. Are you kidding me? A leash? Such poshness was unheard of, and the occasional scary dog sighting had us running yet again. Ours was the land of dogs with no fences, but there was the occasional dog on a chain—lunging forward with savage barks. Dogs like Toro. Toro once broke his chain, pulling it straight out of the ground.

"Sandy! He's not on the chain! He's not on the chain! Sannnndddddy!"

I screamed this to my fellow classmate who lived a few houses away as I ran, looking back over my shoulder while Toro galloped closer and closer toward me.

"Stop running! If you run, he will keep running!" Sandy screamed this back to me as she ran toward Toro, with not a chance in the world of catching her scary dog before he caught up with me. This seemed an insane suggestion—to stand still and let the mad dog tear into me—and I could no more have heeded the directive than jumped off a cliff.

As I continued to run away as fast as I could, my foot caught in a metal well cover protruding from a concrete slab in the back of Toro's yard. A quick, hard fall, knee hitting first and splitting open in a wide splatter of blood, and I screamed.

"Here, little girl, let me get you."

Sandy's father had seen the scene unfolding from his kitchen window and had bounded down their back stairs. Not quite making it to me before the fall, he gently lifted me in his arms and carried me home. This resulted in stitches in my knee. Scary Toro. Bad Toro. I learned to run faster after that.

In learning to run fast, I also learned to never saunter. Run fast and furious: away from dogs, away from pondering experiences, away from anything I deemed terrifying, or toward anything I found exciting. I learned by practice the skill of rarely thinking about consequences and plunging forward or backward, depending on which survival skill was necessary. Since I held my inner self tight, I felt unexpressed as a result. I am often shocked, as an adult, to learn that I was viewed as electric and outspoken, when what I actually felt was unknown and hidden.

Carrying these sentiments into young adulthood left me anxious but well-concealed, because of my external attack on anything I was doing. The need to be busy all the time and accomplish an inordinate amount of work could easily be misunder-stood as confidence.

Finishing high school with my frenetic nature firmly in place, college brought me first to a university mid-state for one year. I was surrounded by multitudes of people, but the seemingly vacant air of flat open spaces had me flailing for some sort of grounding. Transferring to Chicago my second year, where a fluster of activity was evident everywhere, I felt right at home. I could immediately sense that the city was a place where I could hide and thrive, and where the electricity of motion and a sense of pluck and grit would eventually turn me into an urban woman. Having an idyllic childhood, with the wildness of unsupervised play outdoors and family filling in the cracks and crevices where the slightest possibility of loneliness could lurk, I was still unprepared for living the life I experienced inside my head.

Over the course of three decades, I have lived in high-rise apartments and small flats above restaurants, where the sound of mice in the walls was my sleep cadence. I have rented tiny rooms in the back of bungalows and endured screaming landlords pounding the ceiling above me with a broom. I have carried furniture up and down fire escapes, jammed salvaged treasures into tiny stairwells, and formed my furnishings from things abandoned on the street. Metal milk crates became symbolic of my urban life, and I have used them to store books as easily as mittens, snow pants, and sporting equipment.

My very first Chicago home was a studio apartment on the eleventh floor of a high-rise. The art college I attended at the time didn't have dorms, so my parents helped me find a tiny place where I could live and paint, trekking to school on the bus every morning. I brought my twin bed from home and turned it sideways so it could double as a sofa. Searching for the remaining items needed to furnish my tiny studio apartment, I ventured into resale shops and plundered for objects at the nearby Amvets. The hunt was as much a part of the process as the place.

"How much for this concrete block dripping with hot pink paint? And for this dilapidated and broken frame?"

I saw beauty in the broken, discarded, and misunderstood. Curating items for my transient homesteads became a therapy that grounded me.

During my college years, I gained confidence by enacting a bravado that led to potentially dangerous situations. Latching onto activities that could be risky was exhilarating.

"What are you doing?" I said this loudly to the crouched man who was slicing the tires of a car near my apartment with a knife. No response from the man—just a shocked stare, befuddled that a young waif of a girl would dare shout at him while he angrily performed his deed of revenge. We were approximately ten feet apart, and a momentary staredown started and stopped: me winning, and him running away. When I shared this with my cohorts the next day, they were outraged that I would have put myself in danger like this. As we cracked open pomegranates under the lions at the front steps of the Art Institute, I pondered their words, and a glimmer of understanding took hold, piercing my armor of false bravado. I resolved to be more careful and find other ways to work out my angst.

I found myself playing the guitar out of the back of my hatchback to flea market wanderers at Six Corners, a North Side landmark, and this Saturday morning pattern slowed me down just enough to keep me from diving headlong into a land of risky self-destruction. Filling up my time was one solution I had worked out, and this developed a pattern of self-comfort I took with me into adulthood. Learning to play the guitar occupied the hours late at night after I had set down my paintbrushes. Discovering what three chords could do with simple ditty songs comforted me much like the simple touch of my mom, reminding me that everything was alright and that the day held more than fabricated worries.

I took dance lessons at Lou Conte's before he started Hubbard Street Dance, his famous dance troupe. At home, I used the ten-foot-high wall of windows in my studio apartment as a large mirror. The windows faced Lake Michigan and were black at night, acting like a stage where I could watch myself practice my shuffle step of tap shoes on tile over poured concrete. My neighbors in the surrounding apartments complained, which is how I became friends with the parking garage attendants and arranged to practice my routines on their oil-stained floor.

"Mark it, ladies! And five, six, seven, eight . . ."

Our dance instructor, Lou, barked out the steps we had to hurriedly learn and perform in class. "Turn right, left, walk walk walk." The group of eleven dancers I was part of shuffled about with small movements as we memorized the routine. Waiting for the exact moment we would be asked to perform, we looked down at our feet, marking our movements.

"Now. Group one!" Clap the position and go!

Running down Wabash Avenue twice a week, red bag bouncing against my back, to enter a small ancient elevator in a dirty, dusty building, murmuring hellos, plopping down on the wood floor with legs stretched out in front of me pressing torso to thighs, was an exhale of adrenalin as I took my position at the barre.

"Breathe in, out, up, and stretch." This became my mantra even as I faced a blank canvas in my painting class.

My tattered leg warmers fell as I moved. My cohorts in dance were as messy in dress as I was, holes in our tights, but no pejorative judgment. The only requirement was warmth. Warm the legs, the arms, and the mind.

Dance provided a rigid and measurable platform for approval, where technique and expression blended. I hungered for the strict lines that dance provided. I could brush away worry and concentrate on performing a ritual confined by both tradition and artistry. Leaping, tapping, swirling, twirling—dance organized both my mind and my body. I loved the structure it provided.

Years later, my own little girls would look through my tattered red dance bag and try on my worn-to-shreds dance shoes, long stretched-out leggings, and ratty leotards, asking me to tell them yet again the stories of my past dance life.

I was at home in Chicago and navigated it well, whether by "L," bus, or car. I could park in a flash in the tightest of spots and knew all the stops for the Blue and Green Lines. I carried big canvases back and forth to my classes, and I sketched everything I saw, everywhere I went. Always in possession of charcoal pencils and Rapidograph pens, I found inspiration in the ordinary around me. I loved the hum and energy of constant traffic and the endless variety of people to watch. The chatter of sound was rich and even elegant to me, gripping the ideas racing through my mind. The white noise of the city became more undetectable the longer I lived there.

I saw the city as a landscape of bright colors of purple, red, green, and tangerine, lit from within. I marched everywhere I went. Brisk walking, energetic talking, and argumentative coffee conversations filled me with endless hours of convivial joy.

On Friday nights I waitressed at Chef Alberto's, the only waitress in a sea of waiters dressed in black-and-white tuxedos. They all knew how to bone a Dover sole, and they taught me, as I was the female mascot among the heavily accented Italian men. Listening to them shout to the cook in a language I did not know, while brandishing large knives for punctuation, did not frighten me. Rather, I felt awakened from a suburban dormancy, and these experiences were mere kindling that lit me up.

Being around activity that was foreign to me was exhilarating but did not refuel my emotional tank. I had to find little places to nestle in—places where I could wedge myself onto a bench or into a booth in a tiny diner, amid the cacophony of sounds, and sip hot coffee, sketch, take notes, or just think.

Discovering and honing my ability to be alone and happy in the midst of chaos was to become a great and mighty tool, as I grew up to be the mother of four lively, loud, and lovely, boisterous daughters. I had favorite spots, and one was the Palmer House, a hotel on Wabash, which had a tiny coffee shop where they would let me sit for two hours in the early morning, from 6:00 until 8:00 a.m., and pay for just one cup of coffee with constant refills. I would sketch people as they came in and sat at the counter. I got to know bankers and construction workers and diamond salesmen, and secretaries in pencil skirts, as they would nod, say hello, or come over to see what I was drawing. Never obtrusive, always respectful, leaving each other alone with only the occasional greeting and short conversation was enough to establish me as the house artist.

At lunchtime I would go with other art students to different little shops, where we would pool our change and buy a pomegranate and cheese, and share our meager food while talking about our futures as artists. The rows and rows of little shops under the elevated trains made me happy. I knew each one and would pop into the wig shop to say hi to Tamara, who would tell me about the famous people who wore her wigs. I would sit and listen, sketching her as she continuously changed into different wigs: long red tresses, punk white staccato stabs of hair that were a little scary, and blond Marilyn Monroe–like wigs that required she change her makeup to include black-winged eyeliner. I never knew what she would look like from day to day. She changed wigs like underwear, every single day.

The popcorn shop's caramel corn was so popular that the line always went out the door. Doormen from the area hotels, in their tall hats, would stand in line next to the corporate attorneys, waiting to get their afternoon treats. I would get a small bag for free because I knew the shop owner, who got coffee at the Palmer House each day and saw me sketching. I never had to ask, and we never spoke. She would just reach across the counter, give me a small bag, and wink.

It would no sooner have occurred to me to move away from Chicago than it would to poke myself in the eye.

My friends who fled the city hated coming to visit me, and even my family complained. Driving into Chicago meant traffic and strange parking instructions.

"Don't forget to park on the second street to the right after the stop sign that is the third one before the L tracks. Don't park on the right side if you get here after 7:00 p.m., or you will be towed. If you park on the left side of the street, that's fine, but you will have to move your car at 8:30 p.m., or you will be towed. If you turn left at the tracks, you will be towed, since that is not really a street but an alley. And if you park on the fourth street after the third stop sign, you will be towed if you park anywhere."

"Uh, OK?"

Several times friends arriving at 8 p.m. would call at 10 p.m., still unable to find parking.

"We're leaving this God-forsaken place."

I had to go everywhere, since no one wanted to come to me. Little by little, over the course of two decades, everyone I knew began to be tempted by the allure of wide-open spaces, less noise, less traffic, and stars that could be seen by merely looking up after the sun went down.

Thinking about moving out of the city had Andy excited. He launched into a missive about a store he wanted me to see. He was undaunted by my memories of city life, traversing my past for him, and pointing out my reasons to stay.

"But honey, you can't put everything into one store," I said this with a slightly quivering chin to my ever-ebullient husband.

"Yes, you can, and they do. You will love it! You can buy chicks that have just hatched, seed for crops, bait for fish and tackle, and coffee cake at the same time."

"I don't want to put a container of worms next to the cinnamon strudel."

I wondered if I could transition from heeled clip-clip walking to ambled strolls across fields and small shops that all appeared to sell various forms of fudge. My frenetic nature blended well in a city setting. It was almost unnoticeable that I counted everything, avoided stepping on cracks in concrete, stepping over and around with quick dance-like maneuvers, and combined hopping and walking and jogging as I went from place to place.

The hysterical nature of my personality—always driving forward, striving, never relaxing—was often hidden from those who did not know me well, but when Andy mentioned wanting to move, my mask was wearing thin. It seemed that not only could I feel the pressure blowing up my countenance, but small cracks in the smooth surface of practiced serenity were like blinding rays of sunlight through crooked slats in a broken window blind. Everyone around me was shielding their eyes, and I couldn't even find my sunglasses.

I sat at our kitchen table in our little house in the city and told Andy that I was not sure I could sell our house and move to the country. I loved this man, and I knew he wanted to move to Montana. I also knew that moving to Woodstock was a compromise that made him happy. He was magnanimous and generous of soul, and he loved me. So, telling him at our tiny kitchen table, with city sounds outside the open windows, that I was scared and didn't think I could move out of Chicago, I looked up into his eyes as I said it. He looked straight at me and never shifted his gaze, but his chin made the smallest of movements. He was silent, and then he said, "OK, babe. We don't have to."

Sometimes there is magic in knowing that your partner is willing to forego their plans. Whether or not my husband could see my need not to be uprooted, and in keeping with my pattern of sudden life-altering choices, this was the moment I made my decision to move to the country, where I would become Andy's pioneer woman.

Compulsions

*I'm tired of being inside my head. I want to live out
here, with you.*

—Colleen McCarty, *Mounting the Whale*

Ten. Yes, perfect. *Tumultuous*—excellent. Ten letters, all fitting on the fingers of my left and then right hand—counted out and nothing left over, neither letters nor fingers. *Profundity* works very well, but *rigor mortis* is a problem with an extra space and letter, so improv is required. Remove the space; it is completely unnecessary. And the second *r* is just bragging, so let's try again, and yes, done. *Rigo' mortis*—well done.

This conversation runs in my mind constantly, no matter what I'm doing, who I'm talking to, where I'm going. *Count count count—make it fit—ten is perfect.* And if a sentence has ten words, even better. I remain undaunted by numbers of syllables or superfluous letters or words. I cram and shove and insist on ten, and in so doing, my mind is calmed and I am at rest.

I have trouble remembering things these days, which is why a Moleskine accompanies me everywhere I go, where I scratch out reminders and lean heavily on the pages beside me. But I always remember the number of syllables in a word. I drive everyone crazy but myself. My ever-patient and indulgent husband and children roll their eyes ever so slightly but have come to accept this as a "cross to bear"—a phrase that has one too many letters, so I remove one of the *s*'s, since it doesn't help pronunciation or understanding.

I count. I cannot remember a time I didn't count, but I do remember when I started typing on my steering wheel, all the letters and numbers on the license plates in front of me. I guess it's my mom's fault, since she insisted that I learn to type on an old punch-key typewriter in her bedroom at the age of eight, which I found exhilarating. Chunk and push and jam—like a cadence in determination. Each punch of the keys seemed to remove one small alarm bell in my mind, something that went off every few seconds of my childhood. I have never fully rid myself of this leaning toward anxiety, even as I finger the "breathe" stone my youngest daughter gave me (which I always carry in my purse). Even this habit does not protect my girls from their mother's oddities when it comes to words, letters, and numbers.

"My sweet girl, whatever time you get here is fine. Laura Karr, spelled K-A-R-R, all one syllable, might be here at the same time, but she won't stay long."

"Mom, you don't have to spell her last name for me. I don't care about how it is spelled."

"Oh honey, I'm sorry; well, just get here when you get here."

"I love you, my crazy mom."

"I love you too, sweetheart."

I am relieved that my girls know me and accept me as I am, and I do the same for them. As I navigated the decision to move and all that it would mean, I explored the habits I had enacted in my life to manage stress. Counting was one of them, but I realized that productivity was another. It was strange to me that I craved alone time as much as activity. I probably would have been diagnosed with OCD if I were a child today, but I was only thought of as intense by my teachers. My inner storm, which required constant and interesting activity, provided me with good grades and accolades from teachers who chalked it all up to a child meeting her potential.

"Maidy, ninety-nine please." My mom made this request daily, asking in her sing-song voice. With a family of six kids, laundry was a major part of daily life. I cannot remember a moment when a pile of folded laundry was not sprinkling the steps of the stairs to the second floor, and it was considered sacrilegious to walk up the stairs without carrying something waiting to be cradled and carried to the appropriate bedroom.

"How about we change things up a bit?"

"What do you mean?" I asked my mom, who had her hands in cookie ingredients. I was beside her, preparing baking sheets for the neat rows of spooned plops of round dough that would soon emerge from her bowl.

"Well, I can continue to say, 'Please go downstairs and empty the dryer into a basket and bring it upstairs. Don't forget to put the wash into the dryer, and then put in a new load of dirty clothes into the washer, and don't forget the soap.' Or I can just say, *ninety-nine*."

That's what we did, and I loved it. This secret code created not only a larger unspoken descriptive, but a hidden communication that connected me to my mom. Her brain was crowded too, and I can now see the gears turning in her mind—thinking of new ways to do life, keeping things interesting while doing the mundane.

As I prepared for the move out of Chicago, connecting my childhood memories to moving was a natural navigation for me. I rummaged through my mind for answers to my restlessness. Always needing to know what might lie ahead, I planned for the worst and then fretted over it. I knew there would be long commutes ahead of me after moving, and I obsessed over this fact even before driving the trek once. My design studio was in the Bucktown neighborhood of Chicago, and driving back and forth would add a three-hour commute to my already crowded day. With sleep deprivation already a part of my life, and the knowledge that these added hours for travel would eat further into that, I could imagine being crabby upon arrival at either end.

"I need a minute." Even walking in the door to the studio I loved, I felt a certain annoyance if I was not the first one in. I started my day ashamed of being late.

"Sure thing, Maida." My loyal, hard-working staff would dig into the day, waiting for my demeanor to catch up with my intentions, which were usually good. My staff was amazing in all they accomplished, and I made sure to tell them every day how much I appreciated them.

"I'm sorry I was crabby."

"That's OK Maida, we know you."

Occasionally I wondered about this, but never explored it in conversation, having some trouble balancing my angst with my desire to please. I might have bristled internally over not wanting to be known, but wanting understanding nonetheless. I felt a continual pull to make sure everyone was happy, even if I was a wreck emotionally, carrying the unnecessary weight of the world upon my slight shoulders.

Being a life-long worrier made me abhor confrontation and do anything to avoid difficult conversations, so bottling up such emotions inside of me always seemed the better alternative.

"Of course we can do that. No problem whatsoever."

The number of times I responded this way to outrageous requests from clients put pressure on my staff. Unreasonable demands were met with a yes before I thought them through. I couldn't stand it if someone was mad, so naturally, I became a fixer. Fix that problem, clean up that mess, force everyone to get along—and in so doing, my sense of constant anxiety deepened and broadened until it seeped into all my thoughts, placing unwarranted demands on everyone around me.

"John, I know you can do it. If you just pull the toilet, open the floor, remove the joists, reframe, run new PVC pipe, you can put the whole thing back together, no problem."

"Maida, that is a lot. There will be a large change order, and I can't get to it right now. It is triple the work scope."

"Pleeeeaaaassseee?" I was not a stranger to begging. The result was often happy clients and chagrined subcontractors.

"I can't promise."

"John, I appreciate you. And I know my client will appreciate you as well."

"Well, I'll see what I can do. I'll let you know."

"Thank you, John! You are the best!"

And off I would go, making John believe that he had already said yes, putting unwarranted pressure on him.

I consider that humans live life through a prism our mind creates for us, often for survival purposes. We are frightened, so we freeze or run, depending on our nature. We are shocked by the raw emotion displayed by a skilled actor, so we cry unbidden. But we also control these emotions through a variety of tricks we teach ourselves. I have pinched my thigh not to burst out laughing inappropriately at an event; and don't ever let me sit by my sister, as our sensibilities are identical. We learn to hold back tears, muffle the sob, shove down a gulp of sorrow, and this often leads to cemented versions of ourselves when it comes to expression. Doesn't this lead to the "What are you thinking?" question we ask those we love? Reading expressions can be difficult and untrustworthy, so we ask and often receive nothing, or worse, a bland answer. We fear exposing our natures, so we tuck and roll with stoicism and remain unknown even to those to whom we are the closest.

My emotions were always right there for all to see, but they hid the true nature of my worried soul. It took until my teen years for me to discover my need for alone time. I needed the approval of others, and yet found myself spent from the effort.

"Do we have to stay longer? Can we go home now?" I leaned forward and whispered to my mom as we prepared food for a large family gathering at a relative's house.

"Not yet, Maidy. Go play with your cousins."

"All we ever do is *play play play*!"—the mantra my cousins coined, and something I heartily agreed with. Traipsing out the back door to launch down the steps and head into yet another game, I shouted to anyone at all, with loud declarative sentences, taking charge and managing the whole kit and kaboodle.

Hands flailing, eyes wide, whether with tears cascading

or mouth-open laughter, has been the descriptive of my whole life. And yet I felt unexpressed for all that remained inside, clanging around like ricocheting marbles careening off unsettled information. Being alone, picking up a book, staring into nothing, and counting allowed me to put something away. *This word goes there, and that syllable fits here,* and suddenly I could think.

"Mom, do you ever feel like your brain is too full?"

"What do you mean, honey?"

"I can't find my thoughts."

"They are there. Just sit and read for a while and you will find them."

My mom, with her long, thin face, deep-set eyes, and high cheekbones— characteristics mirrored on me—was, I am certain, either folding laundry, baking, cleaning, or writing poetry in her mind. I was sure she understood me, and so I trusted her explanation.

At the age of eleven, my life consisted of school, dance lessons, and several grammar school friends with whom I played during and after school. The studious nature of my elementary school days was a challenge I took seriously, longing for perfection in both grades and behavior. I held myself tightly but ran wildly during recess, unaware that my nonacademic activities showcased a nature so very different from what I experienced on the inside of my head. Ponytail streaming out behind me, I ran and climbed and sang songs with abandon, yet felt inexpressibly alone, so I sang louder, and often inappropriately, to drown out my thoughts and distract myself from emotions I could not make sense of.

Notes sent home to my parents, never about grades, had me scared and nervous walking home from school. I could not understand my behavior or the consequences, since my teachers liked me and I liked them. Notes that told my mom about my "loud singing in the bathroom," or "shouting directions to the other kids in the classroom" were difficult for me to reflect on, since I saw myself as a quiet girl, living life nervously.

When I was very young, my mom would gently touch the top of my thigh as it bounced in cadence to my words. My leg tapped out a rhythm like drumbeat notes, which formed an arena of order that allowed me to sort through the clutter of words inside my head. This loving gesture from my mother, who watched this behavior develop over my early years, calmed me down. During my speech therapy years in early grammar school, she took to touching the tip of her nose to remind me that *r*'s are not *e*'s, something I could not pronounce when very young. In this manner, she was able to tutor me and settle me without saying a word.

Slowly, over the course of many childhood years, I learned to hone the skill of lurking inside myself, unexpressed until the steam burst into the sky in some sort of outrageous behavior. The corral I set up for myself was to organize all verbal communication into neat and orderly categories. Much like cleaning out a junk drawer, things would get to the point of going too far, so I set up a system. Small containers set within a larger space, and the pens go here, and the coupons go there, and I felt better for it. Bing boom bang, done. On to the next project, or in my case, on to the next thought.

Emotions would cross my moon-surface sky every day, and it occasionally occurred to me that I would eventually have to feel them and not shove them into the bottom of a drawer, only to be lost like dropped utensils behind a stove.

My nostalgic nature and love for my family made me aware of the precious nature of life's experiences. My thoughts digested these moments but often missed the organizational train ride into the creviced areas of my brain where they could be retrieved. I needed alone time to arrange them into containers so I could open them carefully as the treasures that they were. Folding back the tissue paper of past experiences and seeing the beauty of my own personality—ready to be shared as regifted and new—was a journey I felt I must take. Perhaps moving to the country would allow me a window I had not looked through before.

Moving to a new environment, not just a new house, had me question life beyond the observable. My days were filled with responsibilities as crowded as my brain. I knew that something had to change, or I was going to ignite and burn out.

I appeared, to life teeming around me, to be a successful designer with a hint of devil-may-care, but the hidden reality I lived was that my interior soul was ill at ease and nervous all the time. Maybe a move would shove me into a land of softer contemplation and serenity.

Packing

I give you this to take with you: Nothing remains as it was. If you know this, you can begin again, with pure joy in the uprooting.

        —Judith Minty, *Letters to My Daughters*

When a large tree is to be moved to a new location, often because it's in the way of a new house foundation, an enormous machine is brought in with an even larger claw-like mouth that opens wide, with dripping incisors that grip the ground around the tree and dig deep to extract it in one giant, moaning yank. This is the method I decided to employ in packing up our Chicago home—the "grip and yank." I plunged headlong into foraging through papers, shelves, closets, and under all the beds of our Chicago bungalow in preparation for packing. Occupying my sensibilities with organizational tasks sits well with me. I have been known to gather my four girls together, giving instructions on organizing a basement storage room, only to have most of the contents move to the garage in a series of parlay mixed with bucket brigade. Several months later, when the bug hit again, we would reverse the process and stand with hands on hips, wearing satisfied expressions as a more settled series of boxes once again lined the basement storage room.

Having moved several times from one city location to another, I had become a self-declared expert. There is a lot to balance when moving, from truck rentals to helpers, to loading and unloading, to providing food to feed the masses—not to mention the boxes. I love boxes because they hold endless possibilities in small, manageable pieces. This is very important, since houses explode when you pack them up. At first, every closet I opened looked compact and organized, only to become an unending stream of items that could not possibly have been in there a moment before. It took twelve boxes to pack up everything on one closet shelf, when I could have sworn those same items would fit in two boxes as I began to take things down. Just touching something on any shelf made it triple in size. I was afraid to breathe, lest I cause a molecular reaction of expansion.

Our youngest daughter, Miranda, had collections of games that were perfectly organized (so proud of her), and they stacked up in two towering pilasters of Friday-night fun. As I tentatively reached out and touched a tall stack of games, a sudden cascade took place in slow motion as seven stacked boxes fell in a crash. A steely calm helped me step down off the ladder, using my feet to push everything on the floor into a jumbled pile, making just enough room to shut the door. Going out for a long walk was the right decision. I finally did sort through the games, though their cards are permanently mixed—Chutes and Ladders with Trivial Pursuit—which explains why lately one team gets asked questions like, "Which country exported 74.3 percent of the non–carbon dioxide sulphuric elements found in swamp water below the Dixie Delta in March, before 1943?" and the other gets asked, "Who is Barbie's boyfriend?"

Packing is like discovering your home from the inside out. It is almost embarrassing to discover all the hidden items that make up our stuff, and getting down to the business of purging should be a mandatory, annual cleansing ritual. I think a new national holiday—Home Organization Day—would be a great idea. Imagine all the homes across America where the garages would be organized, yard tools would have their dried mud hosed off, barbeque grills would be scraped and cleaned, and basement workbenches would have tools placed in the right spot. It is satisfying to stack the washcloths separately from the hand towels, each in their own neat pile, and to take kitchen spices out from hiding behind the cans of soup. I cannot help but think that everyone would be just a little bit happier.

I took our city home apart the same way I put clients' homes together. I want to know if my clients change their sheets weekly or biweekly, as this helps in determining the number of shelves to install in a linen closet. Knowing whether a client cooks in her kitchen is essential for knowing which appliances to leave on the counter, and so I asked myself detailed questions about our lives to know what to include, as well as what to leave out.

Do we eat together as a family? Yes, so I packed a box with dinner essentials for setting the table, and overnight bags with toiletries for two days so that unpacking wouldn't be craziness.

Our yellow lab Clyde's food, familiar water dishes, and comfort toys—check. Labeling boxes was fulfilling, as I knew that with one plunge of the scissors, I could open a box marked appropriately by room, location, and function, and take out plates, cloth napkins, and glasses all ready for dinner, even if we planned to get carryout from a Chinese restaurant.

I was ferocious in my approach, and Andy knew to stay out of my way. "Come on, Clyde," he'd growl, and our puppy waggled behind him, still rambunctious at six months old. Out they'd go to pack up the garage. Clyde was Andy's cohort, his companion, and when Andy sat down, Clyde would sprawl his large puppy paws across Andy's boots.

When I'd go to check on them, or to garner a hug of encouragement, I would invariably find Andy fiddling with some pipe or poking through a pile of wood, with Clyde's big head right there in the way. He knew something was going on and didn't want to miss a thing.

I could only begin to imagine the luxury of space that awaited us at our country home. Having more places to put things inspired me and fit nicely with my compulsive need for order. Since I didn't know where I would put everything, I packed the only way I knew how—the separate-and-conquer method. Like objects with like objects. A store filled with containers for sorting and organizing can excite me and hold me captive. When my girls were very young, traveling to a hardware store was a destination we'd head to if it was raining or too hot to play outside.

"Mommy, mommy, what is this for?" Heather pointed to a small gadget with her darling five-year-old finger.

It had been pouring rain for three days, and I had to get somewhere with the girls, as we'd been cooped up at home. Piling onto a bus, we rode along, excited because we were going to an Ace Hardware store and we could not imagine a better way to spend a rainy morning. Kerianne and Kimberly, Heather's two older sisters, were looking at grills and talking about what they would make for dinner, opening and closing every lid under the watchful eye of a store employee. The thingamabobs in little plastic boxes—every primary color evident—and spools of wire that begged to be unwound but remained untouched all caused a flurry of questions that I answered patiently as best I could.

"Is this wire used for decorations?"

"No, dear, it's for electricity."

"But how does the electricity get inside?"

"It doesn't. The electricity runs on the outside of the wire, and the wires are put in hollow metal tubes."

"No, Mommy. Electricity is in the sky, and how can you tell it to run on a piece of wire? What holds it on?"

Every row brought a new question, with ensuing conversation. A small bag of hard candy to snack on while poring over aisles filled with hooks and ladders kept us all fascinated and content until the storm passed. Heading to the library next to find answers to the questions that stumped me filled a day with the simple wonder necessary when raising small children. Packing felt just as purposeful.

I had a roll of packing tape over my wrist like a bracelet and a pair of scissors in the belt loop of my jeans. I would grab a flat contraption of corrugated cardboard—flip, flip, fold—and a box would appear. *Brrraaapt!* I'd slap on a piece of tape, and some place in my organizational heart would feel actual joy at the empty box before me, waiting to be filled. I marked each box with a black marker and stacked the boxes until they lined the walls. It looked like interesting wallpaper, and I began to use different color pens for each room. The kitchen was especially challenging, though delightful. Pots are not baking pans and couldn't be packed together, and each drinking glass had to be wrapped in tissue before nestling down inside the boxes as though getting ready to hibernate. I wondered whether they were comfortable.

I am normally at ease with space and understand the nuances of spatial relationships between rooms and people. I can fit out seven thousand square feet with proper adjacencies and ADA compliances to meet code, all while choosing a Philip Jeffries wall covering that goes with the Rohl plumbing fixtures, but I could not understand the enormity of our country home and how changed our lives were going to be in a rambling old house. City living often meant the need to put blenders in linen closets and baking sheets under the beds. It would be weeks before I realized that my compact and tight-knit group of kitchen boxes would form a tiny tower in the middle of the dining room floor, where I could slowly open each box and decide what went where.

As I made arrangements for each item in our city home to make its way via box or paper or plastic or truck to its new destination, I didn't know at the time that we would spend the first years in our new-old house with a lot of unopened boxes, since the house had a host of mechanical flaws needing our immediate attention.

My general optimism could often take us down boggy roads, and coming to depend on Andy's logical outlook on life would be essential in the not-too-distant future. The combination of my belief that anything could be done and Andy's knowledge that this just wasn't so did give a balance to the eruptions soon to take place, both emotional and pipe-oriented.

I think we both knew there was something special about this house, and it was more than the granite boulder foundation, or the capitals over the doors, or the madcap way the walls wove in and out in strange configurations just waiting to be discovered. We had a sense that as we took the house apart and dug our hands into the depths of its inner workings, we would be digging into ourselves and fixing something bigger and more broken. The scars of broken hearts from our previous marriages had marred our countenances in ways that only we could see.

Just as this house had a ramshackle nature hidden behind corbels with chipped paint, Andy and I each had facades we had carefully erected to present ourselves to the world. We sometimes talk about our shock at how we lowered the curtain enough to let the other peek inside our carefully constructed realities.

I met Andy through a work project—me in need of a carpenter, he with several dozen carpenters looking for a weekend side job. The dead of winter in Chicago can be brutal, but even with a heavy snowstorm predicted, we went ahead with plans to meet for lunch and exchange job information. We had been introduced by an electrical foreman, so he would be there as well.

Andy was late, and when he walked into the restaurant, I knew it was him, even though we had no idea what the other looked like. A swashbuckling man with a shock of brown hair that was disheveled, snow already accumulated on his shoulders, he approached our table with a shy look on his face. It was this shyness that surprised me. No braggart here, but certainly a bravado as he told me why he was late.

"The children are on scaffolding and it's snowing." He looked right at me, his voice deep and resonant.

Later that day, I called to ask if he would like to go to dinner "in order to talk" since our lunch meeting didn't pan out. His immediate response of "sure thing" left me quivery.

"So, do you think that maybe perhaps we might meet for dinner on Friday, or maybe not?" My halting message, with my invitation permanently fixed on his machine, had me dying of embarrassment.

"I got your message. I played it back seven times." I cringed then, and now, at my audacity and his sarcasm. We still laugh about it.

We met for dinner, and the most difficult part—since I liked him right away—was telling him that I did not have one, or two, or three, but four daughters. My "watch girls," as he came to call them. My deal breakers. Four of them. My heart was in my throat as I talked about my girls, my everything.

He stayed seated and said, "Tell me more." What a guy.

Andy's bachelorhood had sprung upon him while in his mid-twenties, after marrying and divorcing young. Two kids—one having died, and one still living, though alienated and deeply loved. His reticence to talk about his past clings to him still.

"Honey, do you want to talk about Kenny?" I asked one evening when we were engaged.

"No."

"Why?"

"I just can't. Not yet."

So, I wait.

Although I didn't know it at the time, Andy would provide a more stable and happy foundation for my daughters to build their own lives upon. They seemed to inherently sense a stability he would bring to our home. He was never too busy to sit and listen to them talk about their victories or woes, while I was often up to my eyeballs in alligators. And then there was always the element of love. That wild weed of sprawling heart-pulse that winds around the hurting and mends broken arrows of the soul.

As the early years of our marriage unfolded—four years before moving out of the city, with daughters applying for college and high school upon us for my youngest—we didn't have time to dive deep into each other's inner longings. We had each other, and for a long time, this was enough. As my design business wound up, it applied pressure to our already busy lives, and so we modified our communication expectations.

"Do you want to talk about it?"

"No, not really, I'm too tired. Tomorrow?"

And tomorrow and tomorrow, so years passed with us riding the coattails of our love, which was evident and real. Still, we knew that cracks could become crevices, which could wreak havoc, so we waited for an opportunity to open the window higher. Maybe, just maybe, this move would create just that.

Each item I placed into a box reminded me that we were moving from our first home together. The home where we slept on a sleeper sofa in the basement office so the girls could have the bedrooms on the main floor. The home where we squeezed around a tiny table for dinner every night, with the girls asking us questions like whether we thought there is life on other planets. The home where Andy taught us all about how electricity wants, at its very nature, to go into the ground, and how chilled water is pumped up and around the tall buildings in the city to cool them in the summer. We had little city lights strung from the back of our Chicago house to the garage, creating a canopy of sparkling stars above as we danced in the yard to the sound of music from a boom box down the street playing old Beatles songs. My girls and I had built a life at this little Chicago bungalow, and we had invited Andy into our circle of intimacy. Here, in this house, we had blended Andy's South Side Chicago roots with our North Side Ernie-Banks-Cubs-loving superiority complex. In our little city house, we had practiced guitar lessons, labored over homework, studied for tests, shrieked at acceptance letters, and packed for college. Exclamations of happiness and sobs of disappointed dreams had filled each day.

"Mom! I got in!" Kerianne cried, ripping open her acceptance letter to college.

"Oh, darling girl! Happiness!" We all danced around hugging and screaming. My sabotaging of this joyous moment by reminding my beautiful and hope-filled daughter that we had to figure out the money, so no guarantees, was so ill-timed that I cringe every time I think about it. In her spirit of beautiful optimism, she ran to the car where I was getting ready to head out on an appointment, leaning through the window to yearnfully look at me and say, "We'll find a way, Mom." And we did. We did find a way. We were good at finding ways.

We found a way for sports and gymnastics meets and baby cuddling at a nearby hospital. We found a way to gather dozens of sports trophies, create costumes for plays, and celebrate every achievement, snuggling with popcorn in our tiny family room—six people together on one small sofa watching an old movie, mixing sorrow with audacious laughter, memories uncountable. And tomorrow we were leaving.

We knew that in the morning we would be heading out to begin making new memories, yet that had me feeling untethered, so I focused on the paint-by-number nature of the moving project. I was not averse to spontaneity, but temporary spontaneity was more my style, like dinner at a new restaurant. I could not imagine the new lifestyle that awaited us. I had no idea how country life would affect our relationship to each other, to the girls, and yet we forged ahead. Decision made. We would find a way. We always did. Why should this be any different?

I told Clyde to come and get his dinner one last time in our city home. With a final waggle, our beautiful puppy settled in for the night, content—displaying for me that all would be right with the world, even if only for a moment.

Differences

Everyone has it within their power to say, this I am today, that I shall be tomorrow.
—Louis L'Amour, *The Walking Drum*

"Do you like it?" Andy says this with soft eyes and an aura of hope emanating from him like a cloud of dust.

Andy likes to surprise me with little gifts. His ideas about those gifts originate and simmer in his boy brain. His boy brain is different from mine, and this is why my husband can stand motionless for twenty-seven minutes looking at three pieces of identical wood in a home improvement store. I cannot understand this and want to get going, get a leg up, march down aisles, and that is why my husband no longer takes me to home improvement stores. This man also enjoys watching programs about jet engines, ice formations and frozen tundra, cleaning out the inside of cement trucks, what the ocean floor looks like with no water, how to tie ropes in every possible format, the pointed necessity for an organized system to store thirty-four screwdrivers (all absolutely identical, no matter what he says), and why an air gun is best for keeping coyotes away (we live nowhere near any coyotes). So, when Andy does something to surprise me, it often takes the form of me finding a new electronic device at the dinner table—perhaps one that will tell me the weather report of wind, humidity, and temperature in northern Utah—as he smiles a tiny bit apprehensively, hoping I am thrilled. And I am, because he thinks this just might be what I've been longing for.

The occasional surprise gift started within six months after our wedding, when Andy came home one day with a pair of tiny travel binoculars wrapped neatly. He sheepishly explained, after I looked stunned and perhaps a flash of confusion shot across the hull of my eyes, that these were for looking at mountains. We live in the flattest part of America—but one can hope. To date (twenty years in), I have received: a special container that holds lamp oil, a spool of leather thread for boot repair, wax that melts in the sun for camping (we never camp, and why wax?), a soldering device for small jewelry (I do not craft), a kit of buttons, several different traveling keyboards, a knife holder for my belt (what?), key chains with mace, key chains with laser lights, sonic cleaning devices, garage organizers that include assorted golf club–cleaning systems, a toothbrush clip for the car, a caboodle filled with batteries, an electronic device that stores unused data from old phones, a wall stapler, and multiple sets of scissors that all do separate tasks like cutting leather or perhaps snipping shoe laces.

"I can't wait for you to show me how to use it, honey," I say as I look inquisitively at an instruction booklet for the soldering device.

Andy loves to read instruction books, so this is praise he can understand. He will read the booklet cover to cover and then sit and explain to me in exhaustive detail how to use the device, which he will put in the garage and use himself upon rare occasion. Sometimes I think Andy observes me as a complex being who is difficult to understand, and he is trying to find the key to my combination. My eyes fill with tears as I see his earnestness displayed.

Upon reflection, I understand that these Arielesque thingamabobs are representative of an expression of emotion that my husband feels uncomfortable saying out loud. To verbally express himself emotionally is vague, disturbing, embarrassing, possibly wrong, and open to interpretation. The inability to navigate the circuitous and squishy pathway of sentiment creates the need to find a more rugged path, where he can stomp along in boots. As I reflect on the heart of this inexpressible man, I have discovered that his quiet confidence—admired by me and the girls, the land where we feel safe and cared for—originated in his tool belt.

My use of the term *tool belt* is literal, not to be confused with quirks of personality or descriptions of macho mannerisms or even psychological quivers of Freudian arrows. No, not at all. Andy's tool belt is filled with essential items for carpentry, and I can barely lift it for the weight. There are the usual suspects: hammer, fasteners, measuring tape, and pencil, but those are the simple beginnings of a long career. Early on, he was chided into purchasing only the best hand tools by a grizzled man who didn't look up as he spoke to the young buck whose hammer broke and flew across the room.

"Yup. I've seen that happen plenty. Bet you won't waste your money on cheap shit again."

And so, we learn. Twenty-four worn leather pockets later, strapped around a strong back and slung on the outer thighs of a young man, is a coming-of-age story for every man who has earned his living working with his hands. A fumbled beginning becomes a symphony as an unguided hand reaches into a triple-bag belt for a speed square (Swanson), or a knife (Lutz), or a tape (Stanley), or a hammer (Plumb), and the formulation of the confident reach-grab-place-use-return takes years to perfect. Each pocket, filled with an item waiting patiently to be called into action without so much as a glance, becomes a pattern that winds its way into the way a man walks, the swing of the arms, the tilt of the chin, the road to feeling comfortable in his own skin.

It is these same patterns that can be seen in a young athlete swinging a bat repeatedly, a sous chef placing the perfect pinch of the perfect ingredient into the perfect stew, the drummer twirling sticks in the air and landing the riff with eyes closed. The clumsy becomes graceful as ease accompanies the skills we admire. We know it took years to establish that level of comfort, and we want it.

"Mom, what will you do when you get to heaven?" one of my siblings asked innocently when we were very young.

"I will perform an amazing physical feat of athletic ability." My unathletic mother also had her own desires, not just to be good at something, but to be comfortable doing it.

We want to sing that song, land that dismount, solve that problem, run that race, sail that boat, write that book—and so we find our own realm of expertise. We discover a place where our confidence can grow unfettered, where we put in our dedicated time and ultimately learn far more than a skill. We learn how to live a life.

I envied my husband's ability to live and work where he had planted seeds a long time ago, and as a result, had learned resilient life skills. Even though he found certain modes of expression difficult, his quiet confidence made him a haven of safety for others when it came to conversation. I felt I was a safe haven for nothing, since the ship I sailed—called *Self*—was battle weary, tossed to and fro, and rarely calm.

"I'm listening. Go ahead, honey."

Andy answers the phone when Kimberly calls from college wanting to talk about an internship opportunity. I know she will talk long and feel happy and heard when he finally hands the phone to me thirty minutes later. We chat about travel plans, food, and jean skirts, and eventually wind our way toward the real reason she called. She's scared to take the internship, and I am scared to move to the country. We tell each other our fears and hang up the phone, both lifted by confession. She will take the internship—and I will move to the country.

I had a lot to learn about the reality of country living, and the plunge was upon me, so I concluded that jumping in, much like diving into a pool of cold water, was best done in one leap. I spurred my steed to the northwest, cradling soulfully my marriage, my man, and my girls, resolute not to allow harm anywhere near our adventure.

Moving

I saw you toss the kites on high
And blow the birds about the sky;
And all around I heard you pass,
Like ladies' skirts across the grass.
—Robert Louis Stevenson, "The Wind"

It was moving day, and I spread peanut butter on toast and ate it standing up while I waited for the coffee to brew. Our city home was all packed and ready to go, and I was one leg in the saddle and the other firmly planted in city soil. Deciding it was best to pack up my emotions, I threw them into a proverbial bag I always carried over my shoulder, knowing they would come with me—my doubts, my fears, my worry about leaving city streetlights—but today I didn't have time to think about it. I slapped my hands together as I went out the back door to bring a garbage bag to the alley, fending off the cold. Was the temperature supposed to be below freezing?

"Girls, time to get up!" Sounding more cheerful than I felt, I opened Heather and Miranda's bedroom door and roused them out of bed. Their two older sisters were away at college and feared they were missing out on all the fun. Their multiple calls throughout the day confirmed this.

"Mom! Don't do anything to the kitchen. I want to set it up with you," Kimberly, my eldest, begged me over phone. She would be home in two weeks, and I couldn't wait to see her. We would pick up Kerianne in a few days, and she would be home for the weekend to help me sort books and unpack.

"I promise to be slipshod without you, darling." Hoping there was some wonderment and a hint of joy in my voice, I would leave some tasks just for her.

I was happy that this day had arrived, so I could finally put behind me the anxiety over the move that had been building over the previous five months. When we bought our country home, we hadn't put our city home on the market yet, never even considering the possibility of moving until it happened. We saw a house, bought it, and then realized what we had done. My husband was euphoric— ebullient, even—while I was in a fog of disbelief.

Every so often, I would look at our closing papers just to make sure I believed it was really happening. To fend off my nervous disposition, I dug into the tasks at hand. Sorting. Check. Packing. Check. Now, onto moving.

The front doorbell rang. As I opened the door, hugs abounded from friends and family coming to help.

"Wow, if I had known it was going to be this cold, I would have thought of a good excuse not to come." Andy's brother Jay, tall, bold, and loud, slapped his brother on the back as he shouted.

"Nice try. It's not cold if you move." Andy smiled and jousted with his brothers, using words as épées. Danny, Andy's younger brother, began examining piles of boxes and immediately told us how we were doing it wrong.

"Yeah, yeah, yeah, come and get a cup of coffee," I said. He followed me like the puppy he was, coming in for a tight hug as he whispered, "Sis, it's gonna be OK, don't be sad," which immediately had me heading to the bathroom to dry my eyes and continue my pretense of being brave.

Andy had gone out for large containers of coffee from Dunkin' Donuts and several boxes of pastries—all soon devoured as we stood one last time around our small kitchen table, each holding a steaming paper cup of hot coffee, knowing that in a moment we would be carrying boxes to the large truck out front and saying goodbye to our sturdy little house on a narrow city street with an alley out back and streetlights out front.

The weekend prior, we had moved the entire garage out to Woodstock. Andy had putzed around putting up shelving and organizing his tools while I set boxes down at his feet and wandered into the yard. It was winter, February and cold, several months since we had purchased our country home in the fall when the weather was milder. Snow covered the yard, and there was a quietness that caught my attention as I walked down the long, narrow driveway toward the front yard. I was unaccustomed to the silence, and I could hear my boots crunching in the snow. I stood at the front of the house and looked up at the high third-floor windows, remembering the dream of weddings, grandchildren, and a gentler, quieter life. I breathed deeply and found resilience in that breath as I closed my eyes, begging for a serenity I feared I might never find.

I remember thinking, *Better get to it.*

Now, standing with two of my daughters, Andy with arms around the thick shoulders of his brothers, and multiple strong and faithful friends who had assembled, we began to disperse from the kitchen to the boxes to the truck to the road to the country, where a house on a hill beckoned to us. I remember thinking, *I can do this. I might need this.*

As the morning became afternoon, we were still at it. A blast of wind hit me as I was walking across a tiny board stretched between the end of the moving van and the steps into the back of the house. A sudden step on ice made me lose my balance, sending a stack of shoeboxes flying into the frosty air. Clyde leaped into action and caught one shoe midair. With a Charles David heel in his big mouth, he took off running. The ice and startling snow should have been a warning, but I could only think of my shoes.

The day was wildly chaotic, a sky of brilliant winter blue to begin, and a haze of icy gray as the afternoon crept into the evening hours. Fed and tired, friends and family headed back to the city before sundown, and we were left alone with all that we needed: each other.

"Mom, you did good."

"Thank you, sweet girl. We couldn't have done it without you both."

I went to separate bedrooms to tuck in the girls, something I had never done before, as they had shared a room for all the days of their lives. As I gently closed each door, making sure my girls were happy and safe, I picked up the phone to return the calls from my older two girls. Four girls in six years had them all close in age, but still the distinction of two big and two little had never quite gone away.

"Hi honey, we're all moved in. Well, not quite, but the truck is gone, everyone has left, the littles are in their rooms reading, and I'm going to head to bed soon. We missed you. All is well."

"Mom, are you OK?" Kerianne knew me and my anxiety. Medical school looming, we picked her up every weekend, and this coming weekend would be no different.

"Yes, honey. I'm fine. I'll be fine. I'll get there. Get some good sleep, darling. I'll call you tomorrow."

"OK, night Mom."

"Night, sweetheart."

Andy and I were exhausted as we nestled in for our first night in our country home, and a deep freeze descended on the entire neighborhood. Warnings blared from all radios and televisions, telling us to check on friends and neighbors and not go outside unless absolutely necessary. Buoyed by a moving-day surge of energy, I had spent the afternoon and evening sorting through a maze of boxes, finally hitting the bed near midnight after making sure the girls were content and warm. Four hours later, I couldn't feel my feet.

I had grabbed blankets and piled them on all the beds as we prepared, shiveringly, to sleep in the country for the first time. With a warm husband beside me and a *Princess and the Pea* assortment of quilts and coverlets, I was still shaking and shivering, but eventually slumber took hold. Waking only a few hours later in a fog of bewilderment, I poked my blue nose out from under the covers and saw that the windows in the master bedroom were opaque with ice crystals completely covering the glass. It looked like we had put a layer of cheap plastic over them, with circular patterns in pale grays, like a bad shower curtain. I reflected for a moment that this just might be beautiful, but right now, in the middle of the night, I could only see the cold. Getting out of bed was akin to the courage necessary to perform an amazing athletic feat, like walking a tightrope across a great chasm with no safety net.

As I shivered my way falteringly toward the windows, wanting sympathy and a heated shroud draped around me, I heard a low moaning sound. I wondered if the dog was all right, so I peeked around to the other side of the bed, where Clyde was curled up in the fetal position, snoring.

I approached the window and touched it. Ice covered the entire inside pane of glass. I scratched a tiny spot and saw that about two inches beyond this glass was another layer of ice, on the storm window as well. I lunged back to bed, leaping in one hop from several feet away, diving under the covers, and shook Andy awake, announcing, "Wake up! The furnace is broken!" My husband scrambled away from me as my icy tentacles touched his shoulder.

"Have you been outside? *Jeez!*"

"The furnace! It is broken, and the windows have all iced up, and I am freezing to the death of my soul," I stammered out between clenched icicle teeth.

Andy got up to check the furnace, and the moaning sound came back louder and with more force. It was the sound of children playing ghost, wooing its way in and out of our bedroom and down the hall. Clyde lifted his head from beside our bed, and his collar jingled, bringing scenes from *A Christmas Carol*, with rattling chains and muffled moans, to life.

I heard Andy bellow from the basement that the furnace was on and the thermostat was working, but the house was plunging into the cold abyss that uninsulated houses with enormous, non-Thermopane windows of sand glass create.

Although our February moving day had started out bright and sunny, not only did an ice storm hit later in the day, it was followed by a deep freeze we wouldn't discover until later that night.

The move started well, with trucks pulling in and out of the long driveway, family and friends tumbling out onto the lawn carrying boxes, lifting furniture up wooden stairs, everyone oohing and aahing over the house, hot pizza inside with mittened hands curved around mugs of steaming coffee. We were delighted and happy as the chaos around us developed a cadence that most carefully planned hysteria brings with it. This would not last.

I'd fallen in love with our Victorian home at the first meet-cute, paying no mind to the whipping wind that would send icy cascades to batter our windows. I didn't think about the rough-and-tumble spring winds that would bring wear and tear constantly to old clapboard siding. I never considered the unstoppable, relentless, howling, aching wind—like the lost boys looking for refuge. The wind wound its way around our home, stirring up dust from neighboring trees only to deposit it onto our front porch. It gentled for a moment, then revved its engines into an upward spiral, reaching the crow's nest at the top of our third-floor walk-up attic, layering dust on every window during every storm, shaking the glass until I feared it would shatter.

Enormous panes of wavy glass were everywhere in our lovely grand dame, forming large windows in almost every wall. To create these windows long ago, silica sand was heated and poured out on large tables, then cut to fit thick, solid wood frames, forming all the window openings. Stained glass, leaded glass, sand glass, all craftsman architectural elements that wooed me to this house. Windows lend drama to an otherwise potentially drab interior. With windows, homes look out at the world beyond and bring what they see back with them into the room. We open windows to let air inside. Gentle breezes, wafting aromas of planned gardens, are welcomed as dear friends who have been missed.

The magnolia tree, blooming outrageous blossoms of too-pink petals right outside our porch, brought those elements into the room as we sat down to dinner one evening.

"Mama, are those from the tree out front?" my eldest

daughter, visiting for dinner, asked one night, pointing across the table. We were sitting in the dining room on plastic chairs, and branches could be seen peeking around the corner of the bay window—gigantic petals, super-sized and opulent.

"Yes honey, those are branches from the tree at the front porch. I love that we can see them from here, but it's the breeze bringing in the scent that sends me over the moon." We reveled in the magic that could be seen through the glass. I got up and opened the window to allow a rush of wind to tickle our faces and bring the aroma of spring into the room.

Opening a window to feel the fresh air from outside against our faces makes us happy in the slight caress of air on bare skin. Experiencing a simple gesture like this reminds us of the natural creatures we humans are, and of our connection to the world beyond ourselves.

Windows are almost a romantic notion. They bring in light, open to let in fresh air, and can change the mood of a room. Tall windows from ceiling to floor tell a modern story, while arched moldings across multifaceted windows can show a home's ethnicity and historical roots. While at one time windows could be designed by nothing more than whim and fancy, today there are strict regulations in place to determine window requirements in new home construction, with the goal of saving people the agony of poorly built windows. Failed windows let cold air in and allow warm air to escape, raising heating bills. They leak rainwater into the walls, where mold can grow. They rattle and moan in the wind. I have had clients ask me if they can save money by purchasing less expensive windows than originally budgeted, hoping to buy a pool table or perhaps a larger chandelier. I always encourage them to spend their money on the windows and mechanicals in a home, because the pool table can wait.

In Laura Ingalls Wilder's book *Little House in the Big Woods*, Ms. Wilder describes the expansion West in the 1860s. She writes of her father traveling for days into town to get supplies. Returning with necessary food always meant some surprise delicacy, usually food of some sort. One time, though, Pa Ingalls brought back a single pane of glass, and this memory was so important to Laura that she chose to write about it in her book. By bringing home this glass, Pa could cut a hole in the wall and let the outside in without opening a door. When I saw the windows in our country home for the first time, I was swept away by the old glass, the quartersawn oak, and the magnificent trims, never giving thought to the gaps where wind and ice would find a way inside. On that wintry morning, the windows in our house were howling their indignation at the weather. The steps necessary to fix this problem were going to be overwhelming.

We have double-hung windows: Each sash operates on its own track and has counterweights with ropes and pulleys as its mechanism of operation. The height and width of each window vary, which makes for a nice design, but the sheer volume of windows with failed ropes, broken pulleys, and large gaps between the sashes brought cold winter air into our home. The process of fixing the windows was complicated. We would have to take all the windows out, which required removing the quartersawn oak "stops" that held them in place. We would also have to remove all the original window casings first to get at the ropes and pulleys. If we were going to make it through the winter, Andy said we had best get started. Lesson one is saddling up with stamina as we entered our first remodeling project in our new old house. I was surprised at my inability to face this calmly, even though I did this naturally with clients.

"Water is filling your basement? OK, I'll send Bob over. Don't worry, we'll get it figured out."

"A fire in the middle of your guest bedroom?" This phone call came late one evening, as a client's home had just experienced spontaneous combustion from rags soaked in stain left on the floor, on a particularly hot day.

"Is it out? Good. The guys will be there first thing to take care of this. I'm so sorry. What a shock this must have been!"

I was able to handle the hysterical phone calls and calm down the rudest remarks with equanimity. In contrast, I found that doing this for myself and my own house caused anxiety to well up inside me. I forced myself to handle the problems of people I worked with by stuffing worry and dread deep into my mind's junk drawer. I wanted to have a better resolve to handle the concerns of remodeling because, more often than not, something does not go according to plan. So I borrowed Andy's steely resolve and intestinal fortitude, and got to work.

Following an idea from my sister, I purchased heavy blanket quilts of various sizes and patterns and hammered large nails into the tops of all the bedroom windows so we could capture the heat inside the rooms. Since it wasn't possible to remove the nails each night, I coiled up the blankets as though each window were the back of a covered wagon, fastening the bedrolls at the top with old belts and buckles to allow light into the rooms during the day. Undoing the buckles at night would unfurl the blankets like flags of brilliant color, a little joyous surprise each time. I loved these "bedroll" valances.

What I loved more was the realization that having a task in hand helped me find the inklings of a solution to my fear of what might come next. If the windows were problems, then what about the roof and the siding and the walls and the ceilings and the floors? I hoped I could handle the other surprises that would surely happen by tackling them with the same resolute heart and hands.

Come spring, we'd become an assembly line of hard window-work. Thirty-seven windows later—the wood removed, new ropes and pulleys installed, replacement sand glass carefully and painstakingly glazed into place, oak trims scraped, sanded, stained, and tightly put back with precision—we achieved window function and even a touch of old-world elegance. Now all the windows in our home slide effortlessly up and down, which has me marveling at old engineering that still works. The windows are shut, and not a howl can be heard as I nestle next to Andy on cold winter nights, listening to the sound of silence.

Spring

April prepares her green traffic light and the world thinks Go.

　　　　　　　　　　—Christopher Morley, *John Mistletoe*

As winter began to sputter out, I could not wait to see what spring would bring to our yard. The freezing temperatures had kept me huddled indoors, and a thick blanket of snow gave a false vision of a clean and crisp landscape underneath. As the Chinook winds began to blow, bringing with them the great melting, more was exposed than the daffodils haphazardly peeking out of the ground.

Rivulets of water left muddy trails everywhere. Clyde was the epitome of happiness as he frolicked in the wet and dirty outdoor playground, bringing sprays of spring mud into the house upon his return. We left towels at every door, not only to wipe our shoes but also his Labrador underbelly and four paws that he would lift patiently, one by one, enjoying the ceremony.

"Lift. Good boy." I rubbed Clyde's yellow fur, drying him as much as possible before his own personal shaking technique, for which my best hope was a clean water spray.

I ruminated that I needed a rubdown, someone or something to clean worried thoughts off me. Perhaps if I could throw myself into discovering what the snow had hidden, this could be a day of discovery that revealed more than where bricks were crumbling on our old patio. I needed to get outside of my head where thoughts of work, children, and husband resided.

Since concrete sidewalks take you from one destination to another in the city, the need for mucking about in Wellies is born of fashion and not necessity. Not so in the country. A needed trip to Farm & Fleet had me outfitted in knee-high rubber boots with a shiny new spade in my gloved hand, a hat slammed onto my head, hair in a ponytail sticking out the back.

"Where are you going?" asked Andy in an amused tone, momentarily eyeing me in my safari outfit. He was in the middle of an electrical exploration and was surrounded by wire.

"To get the lay of the land."

"Have fun." My husband barely glanced up as I opened the back door, breathing deeply the country air before taking decisive steps down and out and beyond.

Our house sat on a crest in the road, set back from the street with steps to the front yard. A cracked cement walk led straight from the front sidewalk to the porch, where wide wood steps took you up and in. Lining this concrete path were scraggly shrubs scattered with untamed and tangled rose bushes, which made the front yard appear unkept. Even though our property was a mere half acre, this was expansive when compared to our city lot, so there was a lot to explore.

When my siblings and I were very young, we were scrambling, scruffy kids, running on ahead of our parents no matter where we went. We would go seasonally to a nearby arboretum to walk in the woods, and my mother soon abandoned her need to keep us in tow. She would scrounge for a stick, using it as a cane whose purpose was to poke and explore. This made my mother appear important and purposeful.

Remembering this as I surveyed the large and unkempt backyard, I picked up a large stick abandoned in a side garden and used it to poke around now as I ventured out. Reaching into a bed of thorned scruff with this handheld branch made me feel brave, adventurous, exploratory. I was looking for bulb shoots as evidence of new growth beneath the debris of old paper cups and plastic bags blown into the bushes that had been hidden by the snow. I had a wild notion that I might find some evidence of flowers bravely peeking out of the melting snow.

Every May, when I was a child, my dad would drive me and my siblings to the local nursery. We would peruse rows and rows of flowers and buy flats of annuals that we would give to my mom for Mother's Day, along with the promise to help her plant them. And we did, unfortunately for Mom. She abandoned her plan of beautiful flowerbeds in neat rows of blooms, heralding her view out the window in the morning. Instead, she ended up with a haphazard conglomeration of wildly dug flowers, many killed with the stab of a spade, and muddy children spraying water forcefully at newly planted and delicate petals, unearthing them and sending them flying. This is the reason the occasional marigold could be seen several feet away, sprouting in the dandelion-filled lawn beyond. My mother did get satisfaction later when she would plop a little granddaughter down in a flowerbed with a spoon for digging. Many happy hours were spent in this manner, muddy and content, with the next stop being the kitchen sink for a hose-down and treats flowing freely from a mason jar.

I have often thought of winter as a time of enduring—enduring the cold and wind, enduring the ice and snow, enduring the chafed skin and chapped lips, waiting for the resurrection. I slowly walked around our house in concentric and ever-larger circles, locating glimpses of spring. There were small buds on a bramble of rose bushes almost hidden from view by overgrown lilacs. I pushed through swathes of dead leaves to uncover daylilies pushing through wet, icy dirt, and I found a tipped-over and abandoned birdbath. Setting it upright, with plans to clean and polish it into shape, made me feel promissory and purposeful.

Taking in deep breaths of cool country air, stopping to look up at the towering pine in the center of the backyard, I could see small birds swooping overhead, and later discovered they were bats. Learning that they were fantastic mosquito eaters, I didn't mind. It would be months before we found them diving downward in our third-floor walk-up attic, and I took offense. Absolutely not. Stay outside where you belong and do your job.

I turned my attention to the house and stood back, at various angles, to assess the condition of the exterior. What was beautiful to our naïve eyes eight months ago could now be seen as a sagging front porch, railings askew, spotted ceilings, and floors of scuffed old boards. Dark gray-blue siding that had had a once-over for selling quickly now appeared as worn as I was certain this century-old clapboard covering felt. High eaves with carved corbels had peeling paint that tendrilled sad and forlorn toward the second-story rooflines. Portions of rotted wood were visible below the porch deck, and the support column at the back entrance made me nervous. It was apparent that spring brought more than good omens, and we had our work cut out for us.

"Honey, come out here. The house looks sad."

"A house can't look sad."

"Well, then it looks tired."

Andy agreed with me but maintained his ability to stay positive in critical moments of my dismay.

"We'll get to it eventually."

"Are you sure?"

"Yes. Write it down and you will have started."

He was right, of course. Writing it down helped me organize my inner self. I wondered about the paint curling off the corbels like potato chips, three stories up above me. I pointed my chin at the rows of soldier carvings, once sharp and clean, now shabby, in need of a shower and shave. I wrote, "Upper row of ornamental trim needs scraping, sanding, caulking, priming, and painting." I knew it would take a whole summer just to bring these corbels back to life, but it was now on a list, and lists notate more than a task. The ceremony of writing something down documents, for me, thoughts, ideas, and mindful dreams. They are like pointers toward a future that is manageable and keeps chaos at bay. Lit-up street signs that tell me about possibilities, lists allow me a directional—a bulletin board for the mind.

I like the way lists boost my confidence about an unknown and multitasked future, but the downward spiral comes when they also make me ultra accomplishment-oriented. I was told several years ago by someone who did not know me well that I had "a strong need for closure." I was taken aback because I had not realized this, but upon reflection, saw that they were right. Part of list culture is writing it down, punching it in, declaring a certain position taken.

This will be done. This and not that. If something is not on the list, it can be ignored and cause no distress, since the list is everything.

Returning to the house, I took off my boots inside the small vestibule at the back door, with Clyde in tow. Using a towel set there just for this task, I rubbed his dirtied belly yet again, and then his paws one by one. Now clean, he trotted in to find Andy, content and jolly in his doggy approach to life. He did not need a list, because all that was good in life involved being at our side, no matter what we were doing. Lie down? Great! Muck in the mud? Even better.

I made myself a cup of coffee and sat down at the old wood table that has followed me and the girls no matter where we have lived. Looking out the large picture window to the yard beyond, I pondered Clyde's take on life. His happiness came from being with those he loved, and everything else was secondary, to be endured patiently. Like a geyser bubbling up from below the surface, I wanted to feel this effervescence and ebullience without the tinges of worry that followed me around. It was hard for me to imagine a carefree inner life.

I asked Andy if he had regrets, and he told me no. When I pressed and asked why, he told me it would be like carrying a weight around with him, and he wouldn't have been able to love me and the girls the right way if he did. I could see that he didn't want to go further, but I pushed on.

"I know you have regrets."

"Everyone does."

"How do you stop thinking about them?" I plunged ahead one more time.

"I don't want to live back there."

I reflected on this conversation, which was quite hard for my nonverbal man to have with me. There was a simplicity to the words and a profundity to the implications. I wanted to live forward but felt tethered to worry and anxiety like stakes in the ground. To this day, Andy focuses on what is out in front of him, giving his best, and concerning himself with the people he loves. I am aware that he still maintains a rich inner life—he ponders the events of the day, reflects on his opinions of yesterday, and faces the tasks of tomorrow. He fills the in-between spaces with peace and calm and pours this outlook onto me and the girls like water on a thirsty plant.

I could not have guessed that poking around in the dirt and misty rain would have had me feeling more than the softness of the ground. Grabbing my coat and hat, I headed back outside. Walking over to a small garden area that held the broken birdbath, I laid the folded towel I was carrying on the ground and knelt in the spring mud. Grabbing a handful of Creeping Charlie weed that had overtaken much of the flowerbeds in the back, I pulled it out of the ground smoothly. Thinking about my husband and the new life we were building in the country, I saw the ease that resided right beside me. I stopped to wipe away wet leaves, uncovering shoots of green, and gasped at the sudden and visible hint of life to come.

Town

In the great cities, we see so little of the world.
—W. B. Yeats, *The Celtic Twilight*

Since our house was perched at the top of a crest in the road—an old-world relic—it appeared to greet anyone venturing up the small hill. I loved driving upward as I headed home from work or errands and viewing our wraparound front porch with white and red detailing on the newels and balusters. Mixed with the Williamsburg blue on the old clapboard siding, these colors gave our home a patriotic flair.

We were on a direct path to the town's largest park and only three blocks from the town square in the opposite direction. Seeing a variety of people walking past our house was a daily routine and rhythm that was reminiscent of my past city life, so I relished this regular parade. Dogs of all shapes and sizes streamed by in a trickle of barks, enough to cause Clyde to respond with deep greetings of his own. Eventually resigned to the scents of canine companions, he would clump down on the porch, sun streaming toward the front steps, resting his head on his paws with a satisfied sigh.

Many city dwellers have a romantic notion about small towns sprinkled throughout the countryside, and I had been one of them. The intense pace of city life felt normal to me, but there was still an attraction and pull toward the idea of sauntering through Midwestern hamlets where life seemed gentler, calmer, and simpler. I had the notion that life might be lovelier if the streets were paved with old cobblestones rather than potholes and traffic. Even though I was wooed enough to move to a small town, settling in was harder for me than it was for my husband. I was impatient and always needed something to do, qualities that would not necessarily endear the country and me to each other.

When friends would come to visit, puzzled by our audacious decision, Andy loved taking them on a walking tour of the town square. He would make broad sweeping gestures as he pointed to the Opera House, the old Stage Coach junction post, and the site of the original jail, now turned restaurant, where enjoying a beer and a burger was possible while sitting in an actual old cell.

This square within a park within a downtown was a miniature version of Central Park in New York City, with mimicked bronze statues surrounded by indigenous trees. Pagoda dogwood, black maples, white oak, red buds, and shagbark hickory punctuate the landscape. Lining the park on all sides were fragrant lilacs framing cozy vignettes where a person could sit hidden from other activities.

There was a decorated gazebo where a small brass quartet played, and it was here the mayor made speeches on important issues such as the renovation of the movie theatre or information on forthcoming Christmas decorations soon to grace the streets. High school girls met their boyfriends in the square, elderly gentlemen searched for hard candy from a paper bag while sitting on a bench, and little girls could be seen licking an ice cream cone while dogs on leashes led their owners around the perimeter.

Tuesday and Saturday mornings in the summer were reserved for the farmers market, when little booths were sprinkled around the square from Memorial Day through Labor Day. Local produce, having become the necessity of a stable life to me now, had me looking forward to conversations about the variety of tomatoes.

The first time I ventured out with a basket in hand, wanting to be baptized into this rural form of haggling, I walked the few blocks to the square to see which vegetables were being proffered that day.

"Ooh, these look very red!" Heartily saying this to the vendor showcasing his wares, I felt this was a generous way to begin my navigation into tomato-speak.

"Well, the Better Boys are pretty good this year, but sometimes the color can be more yellow."

"Oh. I thought that meant they weren't ripe, yes?" I offered tentatively.

"Well, sometimes, but with the Alicantes you can't tell. They could blush soon and then tighten up, being a dang bit too meaty, but if you stay with the Arkansas Traveler variety, you'll be OK."

"Uh, OK. As long as I don't have to travel too far. My husband just likes them red." I hoped he would just choose a few for me and put them in a bag, which he did. I silently promised myself to read up on tomatoes before next week's market.

Some of my most important conversations include when blueberry picking starts this year, which band will play for the annual lighting of the square, and whether the beauty shop will stay open through the holidays. Starting in late spring, running through summer and into fall, there is always music being played in the square by a folk singer waiting to be discovered. Whatever happens here can be heard from our house, and we have scheduled our summer days around the festivities. Lining the cobblestone streets are small shops that are darling, and interesting to boot. Hand-blown glass ornaments, gourmet chocolates, and the ever-present varieties of fudge are all part of the small-town experience. The few restaurants serving food "farm to table" are always packed with dozens of patrons milling about on the sidewalk, chatting and waiting with calm demeanor. No shouting or shoving, and I marveled at the pleasantness of it all.

Larger stores surround the outer streets of the square, and within days of moving to Woodstock, Andy took me to the local Farm & Fleet. I knew it was a store he felt nostalgic about. When Andy was eleven years old, his father took him to a Farm & Fleet in the southern outskirts of Chicago. As a little boy, he had stood looking around, overwhelmed with the various exciting elements all under one roof, from tools and telephones to tack and saddle. Here it was possible to purchase horse saddles, try on work clothes, have farm equipment fixed, and pick out chickens, all in one place. He told me that he remembered thinking, *I have found the only store I will ever need.* On this day, I wasn't so sure.

On this first day of my Farm & Fleet experience, while still in the parking lot, we saw a woman in hip boots pushing a cart filled to overflowing with a dozen bags of horse feed. "There goes a real pioneer woman," was Andy's comment. I rolled my city eyes at him, since I most certainly could push a heavy cart, but bucked at the expectation and measure of country brawn.

"Sweetheart, I'm teasing you."

"I can lift and carry and push and pull. But you better not expect me buy the horse feed."

Andy looks at life differently than I do, finding humor wherever he goes. Whatever life brings, he faces it, not expecting much more than a little bit of fun now and then. Everything else is gravy to him. He feels he can do with very little, so he rebounds from disappointments, never judging himself in the process. I, on the other hand, am offended by my shortcomings and judge myself harshly. Even when not disappointing others, I disappoint myself. I needed some teasing.

Andy was bent on forming a country life, and shopping for work clothes and shovels was first on his list, along with a host of other items he said we needed, such as a mud rake. "Why do we need to rake mud?" I asked.

Shopping with Andy for what he thought of as the necessities of country living had our cart filled with rubber boots, grass seed, small-animal live traps, putty, warm slippers, flannel pajamas, and motor oil. He pushed the cart all the way to his truck, giving me sidelong glances as he rolled along, eyes smiling, very pleased with himself.

Breathing country air filled my husband's lungs with purpose, room to dream perhaps, and the slowing down of constant reactions that are a necessary part of city life. While I struggled to find my place in the world, my husband put his feet up. I was envious of his ease and decided that discovering the town would be a good beginning. We lived such a short distance away that I made walking to town a daily part of my routine.

For me, the magic of the square had to be experienced over time, allowing its gentle manner to seep into me. Adopting an ease of manner was foreign to me, so I went at it with the ferocious nature I had adopted at the farmers market in Chicago. In the summertime, Dearborn Avenue, just north of the Loop, has a section cordoned off for a fresh fruit and vegetable open-air market. Wrestling over fresh cucumbers and radishes is considered the norm there, and gleeful procurement of more than four fresh peaches is a successful market day.

"I saw these first." A normal response at the city's market, since it was a scramble more than a gentle outdoor shopping experience.

On one of our first summer Saturday mornings in the country, I marched my cart from booth to booth, filling it with vegetables, caramel corn, and wildflowers, which I tied to the handle of my cart. I barely noticed the sweet aroma wafting upward from the lavender. As I strode away, the florist called out to me, "You still have a lot of Chicago in you." I smiled, pleased with myself. Andy steered me away and whispered in my ear that this was not meant as a compliment.

As I nursed my feelings, I walked over to the square, where I found a bench and sat down to snap the ends off beans, occasionally biting into one, crisp and delicious.

"Honey, just give it some time. You're gonna love it." My ever-optimistic husband put his arm around me and sat down.

"I know. I have to admit, this is nice."

Sitting on the old stone seat, a lively tune began to play from the weekend's cast of musicians scheduled for that day. Listening, I stretched out my legs, closed my eyes, and felt a little bit of country entering my urban soul.

Space

There's a beauty in the wide open spaces that allows room for dreams to grow.
—Kirby Larson, *Hattie Big Sky*

Having a few projects completed, albeit by necessity and with no true planning, Andy began to poke around the house after we had lived there one full year. I would find him in the walk-up attic, in the nearly dirt-floor cellar, on a tall ladder outside inspecting the roof, or out in the carriage house turned garage staring intently at something important. I could not predict his pattern of inspection, and rather than try to figure out where he would be, I took these opportunities to wander around indoors, uninterrupted, assessing space.

I walked from room to room and started to get a sense of how we and the house would get along. Both a house and its occupants must greet each other with open arms every day, waking each other up and wanting to be friendly. I like to think of houses as living, breathing things, with each room serving a purpose. It is a relationship, the house and me.

Space can sometimes be impossible for people to see with true eyes. Often, they think a room is either smaller or larger than it really is. Honing the ability to see space clearly is a learned craft, conquered through listening, measuring, taking photographs, and producing drawings. I have had unhappy clients tell me they love wide open spaces, but when I take pictures of their rooms and lay those photographs in front of them, they see partition walls everywhere from ceiling to floor, no natural light penetrating the indoor spaces, and a complex system of hallways compartmentalizing their home. No wonder they are not happy in their space.

The way I see it, a house is planned and designed to provide shelter and comfort to its occupants, who then agree to take care of the house. The goal is that both parties, house and occupants, eventually love and respect each other. When I try and share these thoughts with Andy as he walks by on his way to another dangerous discovery, he tells me I might be reading too much into this. He puts his hand up, saying, "I don't want to know," as I begin to explain. He then simply asks me if I am happy, and I say yes, and he says OK then.

But I want to see how this elderly Victorian home will embrace us. Can we remodel her without changing her spirit? Will we like each other? Is her core resilient and ready to be updated?

I am not that different from this house. I have an aging outer shell but a robust inner life where I forget how old I am. My agility is in my ability to jump in, rush off, and hurry up, stopping hard eventually. Not paying attention to the fractured minutes I leave in my quick wake means that I miss moments, and moments are everything. I intuit the subtle hints that lie in these moments, words, and events, and they haunt me as I speed through the hours of a day. I want to know the meaning for myself and my family in these moments. What is lasting? Will my shortcomings affect more than myself? In racing through the responsibilities of life, am I ignoring signs of neglect? Am I skipping the important for the urgent?

In the yearning gap between outrunning the tasks of life and understanding the meaning of those tasks, doing is the language I have adopted to stave off anxiety. If I work at a rapid pace, I can outrun my capacity for worrying about everything, which is what I tell myself each day. But I am exhausted from the frantic pace I have demanded from myself most of my life. I don't want to live in the rubble of broken-down feelings surrounding me any longer.

I can recall moments when I knew I had missed an opportunity—a daughter calling me at work, but I couldn't talk for more than a second since I was worried about something that was certainly less important than talking to one of my girls. This didn't happen often, but often enough to cause me guilty feelings and insecurity. Even in my parenting, I had allowed the hectic pace of life that I had adopted voluntarily to infect my most important relationships.

The spaces of my heart are molded into the shapes of my daughters, my husband, my siblings, my beloved friends, and my parents, who died younger than I am now. I have taken to coloring these outlined spaces with bright colors in my mind so that I notice them during the chaotic forms of frantic behavior I have erected for myself. I mindfully color them with splashes of blush pink, viridescent, azure, and crimson. These are sacred shapes and colors, and it is now time to acknowledge that I am done missing things.

I want to be present for it all, not just with my physical presence, but with my uneclipsed mind as well. Already, this move to the country has been an invitation to slow down, and I can see myself wanting to respond with *yes* and *yes*. Shadowing my mind often is a nagging sense that there is something to be completed. I abhor incomplete tasks, so I constantly review in my mind the to-do list that lays out like a ribbon unfurling into an unknown future.

One of the first decisions we made when we began our remodeling process in earnest was whether we would renovate rather than restore our beautiful old Victorian. To restore a home means to bring it back to its original state, and I am too "city" to live without a dishwasher. I wanted all the modern amenities that we could afford, tucked away neatly and magically behind wood panels, crisp and clean. I wanted shiny new faucets that did not leak, water that stayed in pipes, basements that did not flood, and roofs that kept us dry and bat-free.

This house oozed charm, and we certainly wanted to pay homage to elements that spoke to its inherent beauty, but we didn't want to embrace elements that didn't make sense for our lifestyle. An old piece of wood for an old piece of wood's sake makes no sense to me unless I love it. This is the true litmus test of remodeling quandaries: Are all the elements functional first and lovely second? They are not always in that order, so holding to such a hard-and-fast rule is not always prudent or wise. Andy says I always think everything can be done, and he is right. I am a house optimist who looks at spaces as dynamic and active, easily transported into something more meaningful and vibrant. I would love to carry this same quality into my life outlook, and I have a sense that perhaps this house will help me move in that direction.

As I think about our next task, I wander through these rooms before me. I realize that it's OK to just love something about a house and not know why. Much like relationships, we fall in love with this person and not that person. It is often the unspoken and unexplainable that calls us home. My daughter Kerianne, when a young girl, was musing out loud one day about how she loved her sisters, and she started by trying to describe her older sister Kimberly. As she stated the normal descriptives that included the color of Kimberly's eyes and hair, she struggled to capture the heart of her and finally said, "There is that part of Kimberly that I can't describe, and that is the part I love." Her ten-year-old brain already had it right.

"Why do we need the alcove off the living room?" Andy asked me when he found me in the living room staring at the walls. He had wanted to make it part of the larger space.

I was looking at a small alcove, extending slightly into the front porch, with large, beautiful windows. I could envision a table centered between facing loveseats, books piled up, and I just knew I would love this slightly separated space. I explained that it would be my little reading nook.

"But will it be just as beautiful as an expanded portion of the main room?"

"Honey, I loved this little space from the moment I saw the house. We can remove the overly elaborate trims, sleek it up a bit, paint and polish, and I will read here every day." I clapped my hands together like a little child about to receive a treat. Andy walked away knowing he was beaten. I could see him smile, though, taking delight in my happiness.

I sometimes reflect on how our house appears confident but vulnerable in its inadequacies. It was shy about the alcove, not wanting to scream out its usefulness. Andy and I are like that too. For every confidence, we have self-doubt, and every decision is preceded by a gnawing sense that we are doing something wrong. This house looms large around us and has internal problems that we aim to fix. As we tackle each problem, we are reminded to view this home as a living design where we are blending space with personality.

Gaining a personal vision for our home came in spurts, sometimes fast, sometimes sputtering along in fits and starts. Knocking down a wall would often lead to aha moments of discovery, such as the stains of old water damage hidden behind poorly applied plaster or water gushing from a surprising location.

This happened within the first week of moving into our home, when I couldn't wait to hang a large piece of art I had loved for decades. I needed to have it up up up, right now, not later, so that I could imagine this house as ours. It was my flag in the ground. My ever-obliging husband brought his hammer into the kitchen, and as he pounded the hanger into the wall, it was followed immediately by a gush of water. No bathroom above, no laundry room or sink anywhere near this wall; it was unbelievable to us that it would hold a water pipe, but sure enough, there it was. Several mop buckets and a shut-down of the water main later, we survived and moved forward.

Other times it was a wondrous surprise, such as hidden back stairs inside a small closet. Half of the stairs had been removed, but here, nearly unseen yet still peeking out into the history of the house, were the remnants of service stairs. This cemented our belief that at one time this house had servants' quarters. These types of discoveries, some amazing and some a disaster, showcased for us the past older homes have. Older homes have stories to tell, and discovering some of them at sudden junctures turned us into detectives.

Every relationship, including those with houses, requires the early stages of getting to know one another. Carefully dancing around each other's feelings, we began to get comfortable. If something was broken, we were gentle in our chastisement, just as Andy and I are with each other. We were resolute but kind. We stood erect and determined as we rolled up our shirtsleeves of Farm & Fleet flannel, soft against our new country skin.

Stones

*I do not know what I may appear to the world; but
to myself I seem to have been only like a boy, playing
on the sea-shore, and diverting myself, in now and
then finding a smoother pebble or a prettier shell than
ordinary, whilst the great ocean of truth lay all undis
covered before me.*

—Issac Newton

I noticed the foundation of our home the first time I saw
it. Driving toward our house, not only that first time but
every day thereafter, we are always delighted at how our
four-square Victorian appears to be sprouting up and out of
a hill like a blue hydrangea flower. But the most prominent
feature, the one that struck us, was that the house appeared
to be sitting atop walls of ancient stone. It is constructed
of Wisconsin boulder, a hard granite that not only forms
a strong and durable base on which to build a house, but
also sparkles in the sunshine on a hot Saturday afternoon.
Tiny crystals laced throughout the stone shine modestly from

this natural formation, seen in granite quarries throughout the Midwest. When the sun hits the boulders just right, the crystal veins glow in contrast with the duller surfaces, and the foundation of our house seems to shimmer in the daylight.

Starting at the ground, large granite rocks lie one on top of the other in a random pattern, forming rivulets of silver and bluish gray, with deep purple splotches. Three and four feet high, these rocks build a fortress for our house to stand on. These proud boulders are not only standing guard but also providing a secure base for the wood-frame structure built both on and above them. The large foundation stones, roundish in shape, appear surprisingly soft and organic. Undulating walls of blue, gray, and pink boulders line driveways and gardens of older homes as you approach the Wisconsin border, only twenty-five miles from our home in Woodstock.

From a distance, I can catch glimmers of the houses in little towns that sprinkle our drive from the city, as light penetrates clouds and makes everything shine. Our house is sparkly, beckoning, and now recognizable. Rising above the foundation, the simplicity of wood clapboard siding is wonderful in its linear contrast to the varied pattern of the stone below.

I remember seeing our house for the first time and being unsure of the durability of this foundation of stone, thinking that perhaps it was going to crumble beneath the weight of three floors of house above. Andy told me that what had held for one hundred years would hold for one hundred more. My husband's resilience of mind would become our constant encouragement as we plunged headlong into renovations.

Initially, I thought that perhaps too much Wisconsin boulder had been delivered when our house was being built many years ago. The dank basement also had interior walls of piled-up boulders, most certainly portioned out when the house was built in 1903. They created a war zone effect, with pathways leading into small rooms of various sizes. I wondered what had gone on in these small prison-like fortresses. Additional partition walls, built of old wood, added to the maze-like passageways throughout the basement.

I grew accustomed to the boulders on the outside of the house, since the character and nuance of each stone added to the overall charm. But seeing these same boulders from the inside made me feel as though I entered a bomb shelter every time I ventured into the catacombs. Andy, my source of all trivia, told me that the stone and wood-framed rooms were necessary and not as superfluous as I imagined. They would have been used to keep beets, carrots, and other root vegetables through the winter months, he reasoned. Perhaps even salted meats were kept here in cold storage among ice blocks set in straw. Andy pointed to an old wrought iron door, not opened for many years, giving access to a weekly wagon delivery of ice, perhaps? Prior to our renovation, apparently these same rooms were used as makeshift wine cellars. The empty bottles strewn about were clues, or perhaps a squatter needed a warm place to sleep one winter.

I imagined that long ago, someone had taken a bucket of thin white skim-coat plaster and attempted to smooth out sections of the large rocks. This only made the walls appear diseased and repulsive to me. Large white bumps of varying sizes and shapes, dimpled with blackheads, meandered out from the corners and on some patches of wall. I considered the lazy worker who had been told to plaster the stone walls. He filled a bucket with a tired concoction of pasty white goop and half-heartedly flicked it off a wide old brush in the general direction of the walls. It appears that this technique would work well if a splattering of plaster is desired, but an apathetic, half-hearted approach to camouflaging this resilient stone would never succeed. Either cover it completely behind boards or let it be splendid with all the inherent qualities these large rocks possess. My let's-get-it-done-and-done-well mentality followed me even into the basement.

As I stood in this old basement room, hands on hips, assessing what was before me, I thought back to when I was a young girl and didn't understand rocks or have much appreciation for them. I never gave them much thought until my mom began to call my older brother Todd her rock. She didn't say this often, perhaps two or three times that I can remember over the course of decades, but it caught my attention, partially because it offended me slightly at the time. I thought I brought a certain dependability to our six-children household. Being the oldest girl, I babysat my younger siblings and went to the grocery store on my bicycle for the missing dinner items, pedaling home with a loaf of French bread sticking out of the basket on the front of my Schwinn. I cleaned and scrubbed and straightened and folded, carrying laundry to the correct bedrooms. I cooked with my mother, who quadrupled every recipe. We mixed cookie dough in enormous bowls with our hands, my mom making her famous chocolate chip recipe, me making peanut butter balls beside her.

Todd led the troops with a quiet confidence that I have come to admire and wish I could emulate, but our personalities are as different as the sea from the shore. For Todd's every calm and solid influence and action, I brought unbridled, emotional overreaction. My organizational skills rescued me from being inappropriate, but I was loud and known to blurt out words without thinking first. Todd never blurted. It wasn't that I was undependable, but I was more like water than stone. I was less predictable than Todd and, while I ran over rocks and stones paying them no mind, Todd steadied the shore and never complained about the stability he provided as the oldest of six children.

Rocks are just there. We may lift one now and then, carrying it to a new location as though the rock didn't know where it was supposed to be, but we don't see them being formed. Little by little, bit by bit, rocks grow in stature, quiet, confident, steadfast, and steady. Since I am so frivolous in my personality, always reacting and rarely staying in one place long enough to do anything bit by bit, I see rocks as everything I am not. That is what I love about them. I think of them as standing guard—patiently waiting, content to be used for a purpose of our imagining.

Andy is our rock. He likes the ember behind my eyes and understands that it holds a mystery living inside me that cannot always be explained. I struggle sometimes to express all that my soul holds, and Andy peeks inside, keeping me safe and secure even when I thrash through the brush chasing an imaginary idea. I am not steady of soul like he is, and I often keep a pace that causes a palpable tension. It is as though I get on a roller coaster and can't get off. Andy's patience and inherent kindness help me anticipate exits that I am beginning to see more clearly these days.

The girls sense Andy's steadiness too, and it makes them feel safe. When they would occasionally call in the middle of the night with a broken-down car, they would ask for Andy. He would get up, grunting his displeasure at having to rescue yet another girl ("Didn't I just do this last week?"), but he takes pleasure in his dependability. With four married daughters and three granddaughters, Andy bellows his warmth: "Can no one produce a man child?" We smile, knowing the vast and bottomless depth of his heart, where we cling to his stability as our safe haven. We love his spit and swagger and the gentle shoulder of strength that is the spirit of this man. We love the thud of his boots, the clench of his jaw, and the deepness of his man voice.

The granite from Wisconsin holds up our house, and Andy holds up everything else.

Landing Softly

A name pronounced is the recognition of the individual to whom it belongs. He who can pronounce my name aright, he can call me, and is entitled to my love and service.
—Henry David Thoreau, *A Week on the Concord and Merrimack Rivers*

"Fix me, fix me first!" our house seemed to scream at me from all corners. I did not want to only listen to these voices. I wanted to hear something gentler, like the picking of vegetables—unending work but simple and repetitive. Tasks that allowed my mind to wander into gentle meadows of thought. I needed to push beyond and away from the background noises of city life, with all its demands, and discover how to accomplish the necessary while having moments that would allow room for my mind to wander now that we lived in the country.

I took on small projects, like putting new paper liner on all the old closet shelving. This allowed me time to think simple thoughts that were not work-related, and I began to look forward to those moments in the evenings and on weekends when I could tackle a task that had a clear start and finish in a short period of time.

My mind wandered as I cut from pale papers of blue and pink and yellow, tracing out small scallops for the shelf edges. I remembered my grandmother's pantry in Indiana, with similar edging, and I wondered if this was where I got the idea. This thought led me down a mindful path toward memories from my childhood, memories that shaped me then and always.

I did not like my first name when I was a little girl. As a child in the 1950s and '60s, popular names often ended with a gleeful and happy "-ie" sound. Susie, Tammy, Shirley, Becky, Trudy, and Peggy were musically attractive to my five-year-old ears. My name was certainly not melodious and did not end on the necessary aria-like high note I thought lovely. Maida just sort of plunked down with a mature and almost matronly thud. Named after my paternal grandmother, I could only be thankful, when I was small and unappreciative, that I had not been branded with her full name: Maida Belle. My middle name, Lin, shortened from Linnah, sounded like a farm girl's—which, in all honesty, it was, since Grandma Lin, my maternal grandmother, came from a farming heritage. The problem I wrestled with in my youthful angst was that the image of my grandmothers loomed so gorgeously large for me, their contributions to my inner self inexpressibly important, that I was forced to forgive them the names I had inherited. It took growing up to grow into them.

Such hope is placed on the shoulders of a child when a parent selects a title more than a name for their tiny baby. "Hero," because we long to be one. "Sugar," because we search for sweetness in a child. "Gabriel" for courage.

"Alexander" for greatness. "Greta" for movie star status. And names that sound like law firms—"Alexander Lord Quest Soloman."

Names fit our kids like grown-up clothes on a child-sized frame: baggy, roomy, and knock-about big. The tiny kid with bony knees hears his name called from the back door, "Montgomery Winston, come here right now!" He lopes toward the house, unaware that his name is bigger than he is. Eventually, his pals will call him Monty, until one day he fulfills the shadow his large title requires and casts aside his childhood moniker. I like to think that I, too, brandished a hope that one day my name would turn me into something better than I was.

"Over the river and through the woods" were lyrics aptly sung as we drove to my Grandma Maida's house in Wonder Lake, Illinois. It seemed to take forever to get there, and singing passed the time. Our litany of songs took us from little ditties ("99 Bottles of Beer on the Wall") to spirituals ("I Ain't Gonna Grieve My Lord No More") to *Porgy and Bess* duets ("Summertime") that I didn't understand but loved. We sang up one side of the road and down the other, over hills and creeks with the windows open, waiting for the moment my dad would sing a lullaby to my mom and she would say "Oh, Chuck."

My grandma's house stood on a high hill (it was a gentle slope in the road), was large and expansive with a mysterious second floor (it was a small house with barely an attic space of tiny dormers), and was surrounded by large, sprawling trees where we collected acorns (this much is true). The land of wonderment came from a multitude of treats that started when Coca-Cola bottles were opened and poured into tall glasses for four thirsty kids, with a "whatever you want" attitude from an elegant woman who was my father's mother. She never treated us like anything other than miniature adults.

My grandma could sew anything from slipcovers to ruffled dresses, and her hands held a tiny needle that appeared to fly, guided by fingers clad in silver thimbles. She made angel food cake with thick chocolate frosting, cut into huge slices. Any food she served was presented on exquisite patterned plates, and I never once saw a plastic dish in her home. Glass pitchers, crystal bowls, chocolate mints wrapped and waiting—for the taking if asked for politely, the answer always yes and yes. Perfectly manicured hands with nary a touch of polish but rather buffed, shaped, and flawless, with long fingers determined and dedicated to any task at hand. Purposeful, polite, coifed, and perfumed, my Grandma Maida was a lady.

We were a ramshackle bunch of kids, and when we visited, we were immediately deposited into her living room to don swimsuits, with large towels wrapped and knotted around our waists. This was in preparation for the trek to the lake, where she had her own pier, as did most of the residents of this small lake community. Upon occasion, our parents would join us in the water, but mostly we were left to our own devices, which included walking to the dam and putting our lives at risk. Todd was directed to watch us, which I do not remember him doing. We played at the bottom of a waterfall, jumping from rock to underwater rock, our young lives in danger moment by moment, only to return up the hill where some fancy plated food awaited us. I have often thought about these trips to my grandma's, and I am still stunned that I was not afraid of our ventures into the woods, or the beach, or the dam. I trusted more than my brother to keep us safe; I trusted the good judgment of everything my parents and grandparents did. When I was a little girl, it would not have occurred to me to doubt them.

Arriving back at home, I would write Grandma Maida letters telling her about our dog dying, losing my front teeth, and thanking her for the $5 bill she sent me for my birthday, always including a running tally of how much I had in my piggy bank. She'd promptly write back, telling me about the birds that came to her window or what she was baking that day. This made me feel important even before I could describe love in words.

My mother's mother, my Grandma Lin, always had a garden of fresh vegetables thanks to Grandpa Allen's diligence in this department. Ever the tender of things growing in the dirt, I was sent out to help him weed or, with a metal colander in hand, instructed to pick string beans. Proudly carrying them inside, I would wash them standing on a chair before a large farm sink. A significant chunk of my childhood was spent with my grandfather in his garden and with my grandmother in her kitchen. My grandmother taught me to make a pound cake by putting ingredients into a pound box as the measure: a pound of flour, a pound of powdered sugar, and a pound of butter. I still make this delicious cake the same way.

When visiting, my mom floated between the kitchen and the living room. She would go back and forth, balancing kitchen conversations with her mom about food and baking with living room conversations with her dad about opera and books. My grandpa would take my face in his hands upon arrival and kiss my forehead, while grandma lifted me off the floor in a full embrace. Playing outdoors, digging in the dirt, and taking car trips to Woolworth's department store, where I would twirl on red oilcloth-covered stools at a counter while ordering tuna sandwiches, comprised the easy summers I spent with my Indiana grandparents.

Every summer when I was very young, I would stay with them for one week, my mom driving halfway to the Dairy Queen meetup spot. Once deposited into the capable hands of my grandparents, we would continue the trip after first enjoying a cone dipped in chocolate.

Time seemed to slow when I was with them—a gentler pace, with afternoons spent with legs dangling over the arms of an old sofa, comic books in a pile, reading one after another. I remember these simple granddaughter days, and I feel a yearning that will not let me go.

The color of my eyes is from my father, and my freckles are from my mother, but further back are strong fingers born from hands clutching earth long before I was born. Books read when I was not yet an idea, and music enjoyed before I could hear a note. These are the beloved vines twining around my heart, forming me from a lump of confusion into a woman who has now become Grandma Maida and Grandma Lin. Noble women with sturdy names—I do not cast my eyes up, but rather bow to their beautiful spirits that embrace me as I go.

Underneath

Look beneath the surface: never let a thing's intrinsic quality or worth escape you.
        —Marcus Aurelius, *Meditations*

Building a new house starts with digging down into the rock, clay, and dirt below. But first, before the foundation is dug, a plan is created on paper, and a certain amount of investigation is completed on soil conditions. Once concrete begins to slide out of a chute and construction starts, everything is new, known, and neat. Not so in restoring an old house to its prior days of glory. I lived in the land of remodeling, where nothing is new and surprises are everywhere. Rather than this being a problem for me, I was invigorated by reinventing an existing space. It was thrilling to watch a home with shortcomings become an expanded place with more room, fresh finishes, and better function. I felt like a house whisperer.

I was enthusiastic about the projects our country home held, and as Andy understood the underbelly lying behind walls and under floors, his initial investigations complete, we came up with a plan. This fit nicely into my desire to shore up my own spirit of accomplishment, so I clapped my hands together, ready to get going.

Keeping busy at home meant I didn't have to think about missing city restaurants or my city friends. I found I could go a few days without feeling untethered from our past life if I kept busy. New ways to occupy my mind were found in exploring finishes from the late nineteenth century, when our home would have been under construction. What I learned from my explorations was that what Andy and I faced in our country home was neither new construction nor traditional residential remodeling. We had taken possession of a very old house, precious to us in its quaint appointments, but whose groanings of age could be heard continuously in the creaks of the stairs every time we went up or down a floor, or the clang of pipes whenever a toilet was flushed. When our home was built, electricity did not power the lamps, and evidence of oil or gas piping could be seen in the basement, used to light all the rooms long ago—before cloth-covered wiring for electricity was brought in twenty years later. Andy was undaunted by these discoveries, and this put me at ease. Still, I felt a certain apprehension as to what other discoveries might be uncovered. This prospect was not new for either of us, since we had first met over the possibility of working on a remodeling project together.

My first introduction to Andy was over the phone to discuss a potential remodeling project. When we met in person weeks later to review the details, I could see the dread on his face as I described the details. When Andy asked his crew, not a single trim carpenter wanted to take on the job, since it would require evenings and weekends spent in a mess of demolition, lots of cleanup, and the potential for undiscovered catastrophes that could slow down completion. Remodeling is often met with despair by those who do the work, since the scope can change at any time, making it difficult to predict timing, costs, and materials. Though this project turned out to be a dead end, we did fall in love during the process of investigation, something we laugh about now.

The ever-changing scope of work can produce failure, but it can also lead to new solutions, perhaps not considered until this moment—an idea lighting up the sky of options. Once, many projects ago, I met with a family who lived in the country and had no place to put their shoes. Lots and lots of shoes. Large and small, colorful, and monochromatic, they were piled up like sculptures of canvas, leather, and shoelaces. With six kids, it was hard to walk past the front foyer without tripping on a hard-soled loafer or the tall spike of a high heel kicked off by a busy working mom. In my opinion, something had to be done—and fast. The project we discussed had nothing to do with this space and included some sort of expansion of a perfectly appointed living room, where I didn't see a single child sitting. They wanted to be able to entertain more, so I pointed out that just getting inside their front door carried a trip warning. I suggested we first look at the function they needed in a storage system for the hoopla that greeted the comings and goings of the entire family, let alone guests. By opening some walls, expanding the foyer into a front mudroom with "behind-door" storage and a larger closet, and reworking the front door to bring in natural light, the house worked and gave a deep sigh of relief at the clutter it was being asked to handle every day.

Ultimately, the family adored this new space, but getting to completion was a trial for the family and the contractors.

Dust, dirt, and debris were evident throughout, even though partitions were put up and cleanup happened at the end of every day. A large and busy family had to put up with burly men in their home for weeks, and schedules did not always go according to plan. I had to constantly marry the expectations of the client with the reality of remodeling, and I wondered if I could be as gracious with myself as with my clients.

"Honey, are we good to go? Have you decided what's first?" I asked.

"I think so." My husband is a patient man, and thorough, so his answer did not surprise me. Weeks of intrigue and mystery had been crossing his face every night, and I loved seeing him busy with measure, tape, pencil, and paper.

"Great! I can't wait to get going. Give me an assignment." Picturing something lovely, I wanted to start picking finishes out and give myself something more to think about than the drive into the city and the work waiting for me there.

Andy was basically looking at deferred maintenance, neglect, the shrugging of shoulders that homeowners do when they don't want to face what might be a very expensive and upsetting construction fix. I knew what deferred maintenance was and could see it all around me. I was ready to dig in, pull up, tear down, but I was still in the courting stages with the house, so I forgave her previous owners their neglect. Since our house was over one hundred years old, we felt she deserved our respect, so we walked softly, whispering encouragement.

"It's OK," I whispered as I walked to the basement to put in a load of laundry. "We'll take care of you." I ducked my head to miss low-hanging pipes and hoped I wouldn't see a mouse run across the floor. I allowed myself a certain selective blindness to the problems right before my eyes, even though I was aware of them, so that I wouldn't feel overwhelmed.

Whether I walked up a set of stairs or down another, evidence of degradation was everywhere—creaking floors, dripping faucets, weepy foundations mixed with smells undecipherable and indistinguishable from musty earth and dank clay. I could not handle my emotional reaction if I thought about what I saw before me, so I tucked those observations away. Still, occasionally, something could not be ignored.

"What is that odor? What's happening?"

"Nothing. It's not me."

"It smells like dead animal."

Smells became a catalyst in our explorations. No longer just checking for something broken, we were sniffing and being led by our noses. Often the answers turned out to be the bones of small rodents, or a bird long dead, caught in a fireplace chimney. Once, we discovered a family of squirrels who used our porch attic area as their neighborhood outhouse.

We thought we had the energy for the repairs we could see, and our enthusiasm had us consider having T-shirts printed with: *We Came, We Saw, We Conquered.* Each day something new had to be faced that was beyond our initial investigations, so we noted our discoveries and slotted repairs and renovations into our priority plan. This priority list was about to be shot to hell.

Andy called me on a Tuesday while I was still at work and asked that I meet him for dinner at the local diner. We never eat out on a Tuesday night, so my initial thought was a romantic dinner, unusual for a weeknight, but this was quickly dismissed when I walked in and saw his face.

"OK baby, what is it?"

"We have to spend all of our remodeling budget on doing things you cannot see." I heard the words he was saying, but I could not absorb them.

"The sewer pipes have exploded in the front lawn, the water pipes in the basement just burst, the concrete floor is failing, and the heating system will not last through the winter."

He continued, "We are going to have to lift the house up and off its aging foundation, then bring in engineered steel to keep it from sinking into the earth forever." After a long day at work, it was difficult for me to fathom the extent of what my husband was telling me. Normally, he likes to protect me from any disaster, always wanting to spill a little joy into my days, so I knew it was not easy for him to tell me about his discoveries. After contemplating how to go about it, he had decided that the best route for this conversation was to just say it clearly and calmly.

"I'll be right back," I whispered. Controlled. That's me.

As I walked to the bathroom to stand in a stall with my head leaning against the door, stilted, sobbing laughter gurgled out of me. Moderately hysterical, I thought, *I deserve this*. I had renovated countless homes for others, and some of those projects had setbacks from houses that wanted to be left alone. Perhaps this was payback? Houses were often content to lie in their misery until we arrived to wake them up from their ill-fitted hibernation. Or maybe our house had its own pent-up frustrations and wanted to get on with it, expunging all the anxiety from things that had needed fixing for a long time.

With my forehead against the cold gray metal of the bathroom stall, I had visions of past kitchen pipes splaying water when a nail gun riveted into them unknowingly. I recalled slabs of marble falling off trucks as though the house knew we didn't like its bathroom and was offended. I saw buckets of paint spilling onto white carpeting and the fire that started for no reason at all in the middle of the wood floor staining process.

I left the bathroom and walked toward the booth where my husband was sitting patiently, gaining a semblance of composure that surprised me. I felt that I should have known. A born romantic about all things, my broad-brush dreams always loomed larger than the reality around me.

"OK babe—let's get to it." Deciding to be brave, I thought this might be my pioneer woman moment.

"You OK?" Andy's eyes spoke more than his words.

My chin quivered, but I managed a weak smile.

We finished our meal silently. I could feel Andy glancing up at me to make sure I was alright. We resigned ourselves to years rather than months of renovations.

As we walked home, up the hill to our future, I thought about the connection I felt to this house, to my life, our lives. I had old emotional parts that were cracks in my own foundation. Little bothersome thoughts had set up camp: insecurity, doubt, and a nature hell-bent on work. Unlocking the door, turning on the lights, with quietness all around, I could sort out my plans for the day uninterrupted. If anyone else walked in shortly after this, I felt disappointed, knowing I would have to interact with them and be "on." I placed enormous pressure on myself, but it was all my own doing.

"Honey, do you love this house?" Andy asked me tentatively. The blocks from the square to our house were lined with beautiful trees, moonlight splaying through the branches, and we held hands as we walked. We knew that Clyde was waiting for us at home, and we both loved his exuberant greeting we would surely hear shortly.

"Yes, sweetheart. I do love our house." My hand gripped his hand tighter, and I couldn't say more just yet. I needed time to let go of a few things that were blocking my mind. I didn't know how to free myself from doubts. But the doubts were about myself, not our house.

My family and friends have always told me that I have a light inside of me, an energy that is compelling and irresistible. I wondered if there was a limit to my enthusiasm. Was my light darkening? Could I only handle a certain number of crises, and was I reaching the top of this bell curve, ready to slide into the abyss of despair? I knew I couldn't continually hold myself together with a waning energy and the emotional duct tape I kept near, even if I thought I was chugging my way up the track of improvement.

I would have to go below the surface to weed out the elements choking the joyful life out of me. I knew Andy could see the worry in my eyes, even when I could barely check in with my inner self. The core of my personality—rather than safely bringing me into the land of accomplishment and self-satisfaction, both areas I had fought for most of my life—was now leading me down a road that felt more like a treadmill of emotional abandonment. I would get on and get off in the exact same place, focusing on work, never letting up, never giving an inch, and as a result, folding inward rather than petal-pushing outward into gladness.

There were so many elements adding to my anxiety that went beyond my normal tendencies and triggers: daughters growing into women, college costs, multiple locations for my business, all accruing toward financial pressures I could feel but rarely spoke about. My solution to most things was to work harder, longer, rarely coming up for air. *Just keep going*—that was my inner mantra. I was beginning to reflect on the fact that this driven part of my personality had been evident even when I was a young girl, and in recognizing this, I hoped to find a way to get off the Ferris wheel without tumbling into injuring myself or my family.

When I was in high school, I sewed a lot of my own clothes, tutored by my grandmother who was a skillful seamstress. I kept a little notebook, three inches square, where I wrote down the outfits I wore each day. I had self-determined a rotation of three weeks before I could repeat an outfit, and I always created one special ensemble that could not be worn that school year until the first day it snowed. My freshman year, no one knew about this, of course. But when the first day of snow came and I wore a short, bright red corduroy sheath dress, perfectly tailored with gold buttons, with a navy-blue bodysuit beneath and a crafted matching beret, my secret was out. Each subsequent year brought brighter, more embellished outfits, coming to be known accurately as "Maida's Snow Dress." I liked the anticipation of this, the accomplishment of it, and I am sure, the attention as well.

I consider this time in my life and see my desire for affirmation. Since my impetuous nature couldn't wait for it to come organically, I manufactured an event I could control, one where I could gain the recognition I yearned for from my school friends. Now, as an adult woman with grown children, I realized that this desire had never left me. The only differences were the faster pace and higher stakes. I had to get off the conveyor belt and find rest in the affirmations that were all around me.

For a long time, I was unable to verbally express all these thoughts, which was unusual for a chatterbox like me. Andy's patience and calm manner gave me room to reflect, which at first, I did not know I needed. An inner longing lingered in the back alcoves of my soul, where I looked for a place to develop new and gentler ways of being.

I hoped that moving to the country, and the intimacy of doing life together in a new rural environment, could remodel the broken boards of my inner mental framework. Each day, during my long drive to and from the city, I started taking time to examine who I had been and who I had become. Yes, I'd struggled with anxiety since I was very young, and yes, I was certain I'd had enough compulsive habits to merit some sort of diagnosis. But I also grew up surrounded by love. My childhood was filled with parents and siblings I adored, and though we were imperfect (aren't we all?), we came from intentionality, with consideration built into our lives. I knew that if I could tap into those roots, I could find a way to settle my soul and simplify my life.

Sometimes I felt that my design company had taken over every facet of my existence, from the moment I woke until the moment I went to bed, and I barely had time or room to think about anything else. It felt oppressive. At first, I couldn't admit this; even saying it out loud to myself felt like a betrayal of all that I had worked for. But I knew I had to change the dynamic of my own expectations.

I began to take long walks with Clyde, forcing myself to meander with no deadline or destination. Breathe in. Breathe out. Time to think, and also to let thoughts go. Time that had no goal or endpoint.

"Who's my good boy?" Clyde would waggle a response as he sniffed every shrub and tree we passed—delighted and unaware of Mommy's new plan, as long as it meant a leash and a walk.

"Make your face small," I would instruct him, as he folded his ears back so I could slip the collar on. These walks became a starting point for me to collect my thoughts and compartmentalize the problems of the day, putting things in perspective. *I am alive. The girls are happy. Andy loves me.* Each evening before dinner, out we'd go—waggle waggle walk— and what started as determined steps, firmly placing my feet on concrete, became, one hour later, soft stutter steps in the grass: pausing, pondering, praising.

I would take these walks without Andy most of the time, leaving him home exploring, analyzing problems, coming up with solutions, and ready to talk about his discoveries upon our return. The sound of us walking up the steps would bring Andy out to the front porch, standing wide-legged, smiling, and bending down to ruffle Clyde's ears as he slumped onto the old porch floor with a muffled thud.

"I wanna show you something."

"OK, honey, let me put the leash away."

"You're gonna love it." As Andy took my hand, he guided me to a small room we had planned to turn into a pantry. Inside, he had cut a hole in the wall and removed a section of wood lath and plaster. Several layers of old wall covering were exposed, and the earliest layer had peeled back to reveal the face of a monkey wearing a bright red hat.

"I love it," I told him.

Andy knew I would harvest a few of the images he'd found. He didn't know at the time that I would eventually frame them and place them on a wall in the future, larger coat closet—next to a mirror where guests could see their reflection while taking off their coats—but he imagined I would be delighted, and he was right.

Our adventures were only beginning, and I was learning ways to settle my soul. We had many years of hard work before us, but taking simple moments to stop and not think were lessons I was learning as one day became another.

"Come here." Taking Andy's hand, I led him back outside to the porch and the swing, where we sat and didn't talk for a while. Often altering his course to meet mine, he took both of my hands in one of his, pushing the swing gently with his strong legs, sensing my general angst and knowing there were some things I had to figure out for myself.

Good Common Sense

It has always seemed to me that the best symbol of common sense was a bridge.
—Franklin D. Roosevelt, *Roosevelt's Foreign Policy, 1933–1941*

I hold fast to the belief that houses are meant to surprise and delight their occupants. Finding out what those elements of delight are going to be is step one in defining a remodeling scope. When I first meet with a client to discuss their project, I like to ask, "What are your dreams? What kind of life do you envision in this space?" Once answered, I move forward into more pointed questions about family members, entertaining, patterns of living, and budget, but I always start with the dream. Having a dream, a vision, is important to the success of a house remodel. Everything will not go perfectly once construction starts, and the dream keeps the monsters of discouragement at bay.

I was well-versed in loving portions of my job: seeing the anticipation in the eyes of my clients, watching a kitchen change from a nonfunctional space to a busy hub where a family can gather, the delight on kids' faces when they see their playroom transformed. But when this multiplied over and over again, layered one project on top of another, I would become stressed and occupied with the minutiae of keeping the company going, and lose sight of the dream state of design.

A house is a world away from a home, and it is my job to uncover these differences and then execute the process toward the desired result of living in a space that is functional and beautiful. Interior finishes are exciting, and can even be mind-blowing, but before pink silk moiré wall covering can adorn a powder room ceiling, houses are supposed to make sense. A doorknob is expected to be in the right place, and when it is not, we balk with snorts of indignation and feel annoyed that the door has somehow disappointed us. Unfortunately, we are habitual people, and so we continue to open doors with ill-placed entrance knobs and move on to the next violation to our ergonomic senses. Just as Rob Petrie dodged the ill-placed ottoman, we learn to bob and weave our way around the hazards in our homes. I work in an arena where people are fighting with their houses, and the houses are often winning.

Andy and I labor each day to solve problems for clients who live in unworkable homes, and I have spent the better part of thirty years moving walls that are in the wrong place and lifting light fixtures that hit you in the head. Who hasn't been in a home where you must do a full turnaround in the bathroom and step out of the way of the toilet to close the door? All this to get a little privacy. Step in, lurch around bowl, shimmy past sink, reach over toilet to close door, and reverse process when leaving. Houses often need instruction booklets with warnings that should be posted: Look, listen, and proceed with caution!

I was determined to lift our Victorian four-square out of its dysfunction, even though, apparently, our house didn't know it was miserable. It seemed happy enough with its rotting wood beams and stairs where it was possible to fall to one's death and strike one's head at the same time. I clung to the belief that eventually it would appreciate the gracious living that good design can bring, and so we moved forward with our plans. Gracious living. What a thought. What a goal. So very opposite of the personality residing behind my eyes. Intensity, yes—but the grace and poise I desired, the external observations formed from a peaceful mind, I knew were forced.

Even though I was excited to start fixing parts of our home that would bring better function and a semblance of dignity to its inherent charm, a pebble of worry lingered somewhere in my thinking. A gnawing sense of dread would emerge at every new juncture because I always thought I might do something wrong. No one was pressing me for perfection, and I did realize that this pressure and drive for constant performance were self-propelling and self-originating. I had spent the better part of life trying to ignore this or keep it at bay. I would pray for inner peace, with no time for the bigger picture, because there was always something urgent to attend to. I had let my business grow beyond my capabilities, and my inadequacies were screaming at me moment by moment. There were things I was good at, like design, but running a company was another matter. It exhausted me. I didn't know what I was doing. I had no idea how to lead a staff. Secretly, I longed for a less frenzied life, and I began to put my hopes into this house to gain a semblance of personal tranquility. Even thinking that was hilarious to me, since no one in my life would describe me as tranquil. An incessant hammering of thoughts kept my mind buzzing with ideas, but this only added to my self-imposed mental pace. Calming down would come. I hoped.

I thought about my inner need for peace all the time, making lists in my mind, since I wanted to come up with a way to tackle projects in an organized manner without feeling overwhelmed by how much there was to be done. I reflected on my mom and how she would manage cleanup after a big family get-together by using what she dubbed the blanket method. The dull roar of activity dimmed, and everyone—from adults to the smallest child—was instructed to go through the house grabbing things that were not in the right place, from dishes to toys to books. It all went onto the blanket, spread out like a giant tarp on the floor of the living room. It would invariably be filled from the center to the edges, but the rest of the house was neat and orderly, and the task seemed smaller when tackled in this way. Now we could begin! Small hands taking large objects to their final resting spot—a book on a shelf, a glass in the sink, a toy in its box—and round and round the "littles" would go until there was an empty blanket and a special treat as a reward for work well done. It was this method we employed as we walked through our house, trying to determine what to tackle first.

Andy said mechanicals and structure had to come first, and it was hard to push back against this. I wanted to change so many things—but what went on the blanket? Moving the powder room to a different location, changing the stairs to the lower level, and raising the ceiling in the dining room would all have to wait. The blanket had to hold things like dependable electricity and water pipes that would not corrode to the point of bursting. Falling stone walls that could hurt someone walking past the house had to be considered, as well as walls with no insulation and windows that leaked. I wondered aloud whether the house would care that we were going to gut her like a fish.

"Will it hurt?"

"Yes, it will hurt," Andy said, never one to minimize the truth.

I admit that I did feel as though I was parenting my house in those early years of renovation. I feared these were the toddler years of bad attitude, when the house did not appreciate the guidance Andy and I brought. Each groan of a long, old nail slowly arching out of a stair tread sounded like a mournful cry to be left alone. I had been a mom for too long to pay this any mind. Out came the nail, plopped with a ping into an empty coffee can, and on to the next tread. I like to think that our house grew to appreciate us though, as later each night we would pound those same nails straight and use them to anchor the new stairs in place. I could only hope that eventually we would be friends and that a mutual respect would begin to grow.

Andy is a calm man, gentle in his gruffly attractive approach to life. He calmed me down when I was scared and comforted me when I sobbed over the enormity of our dreams. The combination of his temperament mixed with my hair-on-fire overreaction formed a great alliance from which to deal with the discoveries in our house. So, with some semblance of tempered exuberance in my eyes and determination in Andy's soul, we plunged headlong into the unknown warfare of very old house remodeling. And, resisting a result much like Lot's wife, we would not look back.

I knew we had to lift our house out of its misery and form an alliance in rehabilitation. I was on this same journey, and if I could ask our house to march forward toward a place of newness in her inner working parts, I could do the same—gutted from the inside, for a new result that just might prove glorious.

Current

Electricity is really just organized lightning.
      —George Carlin, *Napalm and Silly Putty*

Our Victorian four-square house was built three years after my maternal grandfather was born in 1900. Allan Wing was a man who loved to putter, and I remember spending countless hours as a little girl sitting on an old stool in the garage watching him make little windmills. He would take very thin pieces of wood veneer and fold them origami style, forming a little wind instrument that I could hold in my hand and blow on to make it turn and spin. Grandpa Allan would plant these around his garden, and we would watch them turn round and round in the breeze. Looking out a window at his garden, it appeared to my little-girl eyes that dancing ladies spun among the tomato plants.

My grandmother would make gingersnap cookies, which were Grandpa's favorites, and so I grew to love them too. Spending a week every summer at their Indiana home, running with hair untied and unbraided, barefoot often and carefree always, taught me that fun could be had without my multitude of siblings present. At the end of the week, I missed everyone and was ready to go home, but at the beginning and middle, I was enthralled with the simplicity that silence brought to the landscape. There were butterflies to catch, lighting bugs to chase, beans to pick and snap, and an annual train ride that carried me and my grandmother to a larger town nearby. Looking in the windows of little shops at trinkets sparkling at me, hoping that perhaps we would go inside but never asking, I cherished this annual trip. I was all dressed up, holding my grandma's hand, and I remember the tranquility I felt when strolling with no destination.

I never paid much attention to my grandparents' house because the only thing that mattered to me was that they lived there. As I would sit by either grandparent, chattering on about something I thought important, they listened to me patiently, murmuring words of encouragement. Eventually, I would quiet down when enough words had been spent, and we would nestle in to watch a variety show on their old television.

Looking around the room at the simple decorations, I did notice the electrical wiring in their house because it could be seen outside the walls. Vertical patterns of soft brown cloth that looked to me like shoelaces wound their way over round white knobs attached high at the ceiling. My grandparents told me not to touch when I asked about these gentle arcs of cord, and so I respectfully did not, but I did look suspiciously at the apparatus. Little did I know that this same system of bringing electrical current into their house would grace my own home fifty years later.

The discovery of knob-and-tube electrical wiring in our attic mystified me a bit but filled Andy with the kind of excitement a scary movie brings when the main character ventures down the dark stairway into the cellar.

"Don't go down there!"

But down they go, and up went my husband to the attic, grabbing ceramic knobs once he got there. The same brown fabric I remembered covered the white knobs, acting as the only insulation over the wires that brought electricity into our home. I could still hear my grandmother telling me not to touch.

I feared Andy would electrocute himself and told him so. He explained enthusiastically that the voltage from Eureba's circuit, on the land of Mars, had ventrilocuted the ceramic orbs from the cloth ventricles of lantropin, and that everything should be OK for now. I nodded knowingly, having learned to limit my questions about electricity.

Once, many years ago, at the start of a road trip during an electrical storm and rain deluge, I asked Andy about lightning rods. Why were they mounted on the tops of open field structures and large houses in the country? I had a basic understanding that the rod took the hit for the house, but how did the lightning *know* to do this? He patiently explained that lightning, like all electricity, wants to go to the ground, as though that was obvious and explained everything. I made the mistake of then asking him why, and he spent the duration of our four-hour drive to Michigan talking about opposing charges, storm clouds, and stepped leaders, and how the lightning we see actually comes from the ground, not the sky. That's when I knew he was making it up and stopped listening. Three days later, as we began the drive home, I asked:

"If the lightning I see comes from the ground and goes up, then why do you need lightning rods? And how come a tree doesn't explode from the root?"

"Stop. I don't want to talk about it."

As Andy continued his electrical inspections in the attic, I asked him whether all the electricity in our house was like this. He told me yes, and that we had to rip open the walls in our gracious grand dame, gutting her like a large trout. I sighed at yet another roadblock in my plans for beautiful finishes. I reminded myself that good design seen on the outside reflects a good foundation on the inside. I have marveled over the years at how much work goes into building a home before any drywall is hung. Building on paper is one thing, but actual construction begins with an undergirding that allows everything else to drape nicely, unpuckered and smooth.

There is a broad hallway at the second-floor landing of our home that contains a few small doors in the walls, each carefully trimmed with elegant moldings and antique brass fittings. These little doors open to expose unusual electrical connections that at first appeared mystifying, then terrifying. I was amazed that electrocution could be so easily available.

"Rip it all out," Andy, ever the contractor, dismissed with a wave of his rugged hands. I stood my ground on keeping the little doors.

"No way! These are magical little doors." Resolute in my desire to keep what I saw as part of the personality of the house, Andy was equally resolute in his desire to make the electrical system work a bit easier.

"There is no magic in our hallway." Andy was immovable and unwavering.

"Yes, baby! It is magic when you open them. You expect something to be in there. You want something to be in there."

"I don't want anything to be in there. We need to rip it all out and plaster over the opening. The door won't matter when the old wiring is gone."

"Nooooo." I made fists, rubbing my eyes, taking a moment to let this conversation kick into gear. I stood firm and, looking up straight into my husband's eyes, I said again, "No."

Andy was taken aback. It is rare that I dig my heels in. This was different than deciding to move. This was small to Andy and big to me. When it was big to Andy and big to me, we could talk and find common ground. But here, in this moment, where charm mattered to me, I held fast to this visceral, though emotional, decision regarding a seemingly small element. I had fallen in love with this house partly for its quirks and cavities, and I wasn't going to let this one slip away.

I think I was adamant that the small doors remain since they reminded me of the need to find delight in small spaces. Andy relented, saying he "gave up," but he knew this was a sore spot for me. It was the small things I could focus on—that I needed to focus on. I knew the largeness of the reward upon opening these doors.

I redesigned these little alcoves into hidden spaces that open to surprises, with unusual wall coverings inside each—chuffed birds sitting on perches, proud and puffed, and a large bougainvillea in another—offering a wonderful experience of unexpected discovery. Andy did not understand why I was putting so much effort into a little doorway that would be opened rarely. I explained that someone might open the door and find a moment of delight in a small but experiential way, and that this kind of happiness is what I want this house to do. He smiled shyly at my delight as I mixed glue and splattered it onto wallpaper.

"Sorry."

I looked up and smiled back.

Hiding Places

You can keep as quiet as you like, but one of these days somebody is going to find you.
                    —Haruki Murakami, *1Q84*

Lurking behind the walls of our home that was "getting older by the minute" were multiple problems, hard to address. In the basement, there was mildew growing on old foundation stone that required scraping and scrubbing with some sort of acid concoction involving impenetrable gloves and a face mask that my husband donned every time he ventured into the labyrinth. On the second floor, a leak from the hall bath was yet to be discovered, but we had seen the faint glimmer of a stain on the kitchen ceiling.

"What is that? Do you see that spot?" I asked.

"No."

"Are you sure? Look closer," I pressed.

"I don't want to look, and you can't make me."

I laughed as Andy said this, watching him walk upstairs with a plastic bucket in his hand. "What is that for?" I asked as I sat down at the kitchen table with a colander and fresh beans I had purchased from the farmers market earlier in the day.

"You don't want to know."

Of course I followed him.

Earlier in the spring, a bat had flown through an opening in one of the pocket doors on the main floor, traveling through attic walls and somehow navigating into the open space of the house. Our house was balloon-framed, which allowed open spaces in the walls that extended from the main floor up past the second floor and into the third-floor attic space above. This errant bat was most likely frantic, lost, and had some sense of relief at finding a way out of the internal maze of walls. My reaction was to scream along with Heather, hands flailing and protecting our heads as we ran out the front door, past the porch, and into the front yard. Miranda (Mandy), our youngest, calm in the face of emergencies, grabbed a tennis racquet from the back porch and smacked the bat on the head, where it promptly fell, dazed and confused, onto the floor. Mandy put a bowl over it so that I wouldn't see the bat and called the all-clear.

"Why are you carrying a bucket? What is happening?" I repeated. I thought perhaps it had something to do with water, but when he walked past the bathrooms and headed to the third floor, I knew it was worse than water.

I don't like vermin of any kind, but the prospect of a bat invasion was in the vicinity of an evil invasion. This felt personal. Ultimately, we had to find a company that specialized in bat removal, since the brown bat is an endangered species in McHenry County.

"You have got to be kidding me." I couldn't suppress my thoughts when I talked to the person at the Illinois Department of Public Health.

"Oh no, ma'am. We get calls to bring bats into areas that have a high mosquito count."

"Well, you can have ours." We ended the phone call chuckling, and I was happy to have found a solution. I had to run upstairs and tell Andy.

We had other challenges we could see in the form of doors that did not close properly, letting large gaps of cold or hot air pour into our home. This we could ignore in the short term, as we also had to contend with a basement floor that was disintegrating, allowing for moist pockets of mud that I would walk through every time I did laundry. Smacking my head one too many times on an abandoned water tank hung from basement beams had us finally removing this albatross, and we were reminded again that this would be a cyclical project, much like painting the Golden Gate Bridge. By the time we got through everything to be done, we would need to start again at the beginning due to the length of time for the initial remodeling cycle to complete.

It was the dining room, though, that caught our immediate attention. Just past this room's wide, heavy, and thick converging pocket doors was a room we dubbed the family room. This lovely space had large windows of sand glass that looked out onto the covered porch beyond. In the evenings we would sit in here on a very old sofa and watch television, zoning out for a few minutes before opening up and talking about our days in the Wild West of remodeling for clients. This routine after dinner became our verbal unwind from the day, and we both looked forward to it. After telling about our day, we would dream about which project to tackle next in our own home.

While driving back and forth to work, Andy would make mental lists of which project to tackle first over the weekend and then discuss this with me. I loved listening to his logical explanations, reasoning out each factor, both of us guesstimating time and budget. These conversations could become tense or tentative, as every potential project would cost more in terms of money and time commitment than originally thought. Often, I would listen with a side-eye and gritted teeth, gearing up for yet another disaster to be announced. On one of these evenings, I noticed something unusual. I looked across the family room and into the dining room, and something seemed strange about the ceiling.

"Honey, does the ceiling in the dining room look lower to you?" I was sitting on the sofa with papers spread around me, trying to bring some semblance of order to a pile I had brought home from the studio. I was staring off into the distance as if that would help with my sorting. The ceiling in the next room had a lot of cracks, but this seemed a normal condition for a house of a certain age. All the walls had some sort of warbled pattern of cracks in the old lath and plaster.

"No," Andy replied without looking up, absorbed in a golf tournament on TV.

Sitting up and focusing on the dining room beyond, I was certain something was off.

"It looks lower. Look at the height above the windows. Doesn't that look different than the other rooms?"

With a somewhat frustrated sigh, Andy got up and retrieved a few tools of an investigative nature and punched a small hole in the ceiling. A large chunk of plaster fell on his head and before you knew it, there was a cavernous hole showing us the problem hidden above.

"Are you OK?" Quickly getting up from the sofa, I sprinted to the ladder Andy was using. He tussled his hair, flicking off more dusty chunks and splaying the flakes across the room.

"Well, you were right. Something is wrong, and it's more than the plaster." Standing on the ladder, Andy pointed to the newly formed jaw-like opening in the ceiling.

"I'll get a flashlight."

Handing the light to Andy, he peered in and then beckoned me to join him. A strange system of small boards, each about a foot long, was holding up the original ceiling. These acted like braces, installed in a haphazard pattern that I could not make sense of. Several had fallen, and a stained, slouching splay of water damage could be seen in the original ceiling above the boards.

"So, this was the solution to a ceiling problem. Cut and install dozens of small boards, hammer them with large anchor nails to the original lath, and then cover that with more lath and plaster?"

"Yup. Exactly."

We were so surprised that we started to laugh. Andy with his plastery head of hair and me aghast at the painstaking solution that fixed nothing but merely covered up the problem.

Andy said the only thing to do was remove the whole ceiling from this twenty-two-foot by sixteen-foot dining room. This would be difficult and messy enough, involving piles and piles of old, dirty wood lath and even dirtier plaster. But once this was done, it revealed the real cause of the problem: incorrectly sized ceiling joists that were old and collapsing, and would take a lot more brawn and stamina to correct. Two weeks of demolition later, my eyes glazed over, taking in the challenges that seemed to infect every room. I bit my lip and listened to my husband's explanation of what would need to be done to fix this.

"Baby, we must fix this—we have to get this right. I love this space more than the rest of the house," I pleaded.

"Calm down. It'll take some doing, but I'll get it."

We discovered that the large master bedroom above had never had correctly sized floor joists installed for such a long twenty-foot span, which meant that over the course of decades, the floor sagged, creaked, moaned, and argued with the occupants of the master suite, ultimately showing up in a cracked and falling-plaster shower in the dining room below. A cheap fix would never do for my thorough husband.

His project of building a support wall in three locations, then removing the incorrectly sized joists and installing new ones, properly dimensioned, was one of momentous proportions. It extended through Labor Day, on past Halloween, infringed on Thanksgiving, and threatened Christmas. Finally realizing that the repair work and rebuild would not be done until the new year, I decided to staple little white Christmas lights to the joists so that we would have a semi-camouflaged ceiling for the holidays.

"Honey! Come and see!" I plugged in the final strand of lights to an extension cord draped across the top of the largest dining room window. The entire ceiling twinkled in a soft white glow of little stars.

"Well, it sure is different." My delight interrupted Andy's demeanor, and he pulled me to him with a strong arm around my waist. I nuzzled my head into his chest, realizing that even when something is wrong and the first thought is to hide the flaw, deciding to bring it into the light and expose the imperfections can be more beautiful than imagined.

Later that night, our doorbell rang. A young couple was walking past our house that evening in early December, and they wanted to know if they could please look at our light fixture since they had seen the "stars" from the sidewalk.

"Yes, yes, come in!" I didn't tell them until they entered the dining room that the twinkling stars came from a box of holiday decorations.

This large space, even before our ceiling renovation discovery, had formed my first dream for country living. I wanted to recreate the family gatherings and dinners I experienced as a young girl, when our large extended family would come over for a meal. Serenity rarely ruled our roost. Aunts, uncles, grandparents, and friends were often underfoot, and the jumbled chaos of these gatherings formed a glorious mash-up of personalities. From loud and boisterous to moments gentle of soul, I adored them all.

One Thanksgiving, twenty-two adults gathered at three long tables jammed together, and fourteen small children ate in the next room.

"Oh, I'm sorry I'm interrupting."

"Oh, for heaven's sake, Maida! You must interrupt. Otherwise, you will never be able to speak."

I learned my lesson in navigating family conversations. It was the sound of exclamation—"It was not Archduke Ferdinand!" followed by the burst of laughter as someone proved it was, too—the way everyone looked each other in the eye, the slaps on the back, the audacious stories, and the way no one got up to leave, that carved out a permanent relief in the familial granite I stood on. I wanted to form these same dining room memories with my family.

Dining rooms are sacred places to me. In my grammar school days, my siblings and I would bring home papers that would be placed at the right of my father's dinner plate on our dining table. For a moment, during the hubbub that comes with music lessons, sports activities, and homework, we stopped and ate our evening meal together every day. We were a normal, loud bunch of six kids who wanted our parents to be proud of us, and so we drank in their praise as Dad picked up each piece of accomplishment with a simple remark of "Good work, General" to my brothers, or "Beautiful and well done" to me or my sisters. My mom oohed and aahed her way through the pile after my dad handed it to her when his examinations were complete. We glowed both in the praise of our parents and in the comfort to our souls that we had been seen for the individuals we knew we were in this unit called family. My boisterous nature had me trying not to talk while bouncing my legs in a drummed and frenetic pace where I sat. Where was my mom's touch when I needed it most as a middle-aged woman bouncing too hard at life? I missed her and had raised my kids without her wisdom, feeling like no one really knew me quite like she did.

My mother had taught me to accept the two different sides of my personality: the one I thought everyone saw, where I could be inappropriate, loud, and boisterous, and the other that was contemplative, serious, but hidden and insecure. It is here where I needed books and music to steer my soul into the dock and rest. Moving at breakneck speed was my comfort zone to bear up under the weight of the responsibilities I faced each day. When my mom was alive, I found a respite in her voice, her being, her sensibilities.

When my mom died, I was thirty-three years old and had four little girls of my own, my youngest just barely one. With her gone, I felt orphaned among the angels. There was no one to replace the kindness, the goodness, the brilliance of my mother, as I saw her as both a mentor and a muse. Defining myself without having her to moor me to myself made me feel untethered—a sort of floating through life, never touching down.

With little time to grieve and heal due to urgent life matters at hand, like changing diapers, nursing, and teaching little girls how to read, I began to lose my identity and even my personality by trying to become a version of myself I barely recognized. My nature felt like a secret I had to keep, never letting anyone know how out of control my mind felt. As my little girls grew to be big girls, they were my life raft. Loving them and leading them became the pattern of life that lifted me out of myself. My girls saved me, not a task daughters should have to take on, but I realize the truth of this, even so. As each one grew up, finished college, married, and moved out of our house, my mind revved up again to achieve new goals that I thought were necessary to existence. Speeding through life became commonplace for me, a pattern I had lived in the past. Friends would find me unavailable because I was always working.

We had moved to the country to renovate an old house when it was me that needed fixing. Little by little, I began to see forward steps of progress, like taking joy in a simple dining room ceiling. I felt so delighted to have come up with a solution that was incomplete and yet gave me so much pleasure. I surprised myself by discovering happiness in old boards, sawdust, and strings of sparkly lights. Tackling the hidden remodeling issues in our home was a demolition project for my inner self as much as for the house. The surprise was that I was beginning to reconnect with parts of my personality I had not seen in a long time—things like wonderment, and even a gentler spirit I barely recognized. This was a journey that was beginning to have little lights of its own, guiding my path to a simpler future where I could enjoy the company of those I love.

Later that spring, a beautifully proportioned ceiling emerged with carved two-layer crown molding, custom-made to match the other rooms of the house, a polished and glowing Venetian plaster on the walls, and sheer silk Roman blinds gracing the large three-windowed bay. This dining room has become our favorite place in the house when family arrives. Here we sit and make announcements, tell stories, commiserate, and love on one another.

Several years later, after weddings had begun to take root in our daughters, the bustle of preparing Thanksgiving dinner was a madhouse of piled-on love, seen in the touchy-feely manner of our family, combined with stirring gravy and mashing potatoes. We hugged, and we kissed, and we circled our arms all the way around each other, as though we wouldn't see each other again for a long time.

"Mom, there is a small box at your place, just a little something. You can open it when we all come to the table." Kerianney smiled and continued to carry dishes to the dining room. Just like my beautiful daughter, all my daughters, always thinking about me or Andy or each other, and my heart leapt within me at the sweet and generous spirits of the girls.

"Sure thing, darling. Grab the serving spoons if you can?"

The mayhem continued until finally all the girls, all their men, and four of our grandchildren, ages two through six at the time, were seated. We all joined hands, and with heads bowed, Andy was just about to say a blessing when Bear—the nickname my second daughter had gained as a baby—gently whispered, "Mom, the box."

"Oh yes! I almost forgot." I snatched up the pretty silver box (that I still have) and tore open the ribbon (that still graces my jewelry box), and inside was a small piece of paper, now tucked away where I keep my treasures. It was an ultrasound with the words, "It's a boy!" I lost it. My bursting into tears and running to the other side of the table to hug my daughter caused a wild celebration that had us all eating lukewarm food with tears streaming down our faces after we finally settled in.

Such is the manner of most of our dinners when all the family is here. A celebration, a tragedy, a sorrow, an accomplishment—all such punctuation points of life are welcome at our table.

The Porch

There is always one moment in childhood when the door opens and lets the future in.
  —Graham Greene, *The Power and the Glory*

I feel a certain anxious expectation when I approach the front door of any home. The house might be a quintessential mid-century modern with a bright tangerine door that beckons me to enter, or a French Tudor manor house with a blue limestone walk. Gravel, with its pleasant sound of small round stones crunching under my shoes, might lead me to an arched-top door. Tall urns standing majestic on either side of a raised-panel door painted a brilliant blue could call me forward, or I might make my way over stained and molded concrete leading toward a vacation house on a lake. I have even crossed wooden planks placed strategically over muddy farmhouse paths. In all situations, whether the style is contemporary and crisp or softly gentle in its approach, I want to be wooed into the home by the anticipation of what awaits on the other side of the door.

The front door to our home struck me as a dull red surprise under the canopy of the large porch the first time I approached. Gunmetal-gray clapboard siding could be seen beneath the shade created by the porch ceiling. The painted front door was a flat and ruddy red with white trim casings that formed a simple crown capital above. As I considered our front entrance, examining in greater detail this important area of our home that I would experience every single day, I recalled my measure of anxiety at the thought of moving to the country. I remember feeling comforted by the rundown appearance of the wood siding and peeling paint. The house looked a little bit tired, and a kindred connection had begun between the house and me. I was tired too.

A crumbly and cracked walk, which seemed mossy and quaint at first glance, led to wide wood steps. Graying paint on the treads, blotched and worn in the middle, suggested the decades of wear these stairs had endured. The steps led up to the large porch that wrapped around the front and side of the house, where old white wood columns interrupted the length every eight feet. Square columns supported the ceiling of the porch, where peeling paint layers looked like little dirty potato chips. A sprinkling had fallen to the floor, and they crunched when I walked on them. I could sense, even at first glance, that this porch would take me further away from the city than any measurable distance.

On my front porch I placed important entrance memorabilia: an old lantern, a rocker found and refurbished, a large copper bucket filled with pinecones, all items welcoming the arrival of guests even before they pressed the doorbell. I used to think that porches meant only Midwestern chumminess, but I see porches everywhere I go in America. Even in places where houses are crowded together, porches line up in rows like little open boxes, wooing neighbors to chat at the end of a day. A porch means talking if you feel like it. The slam of a screen door when someone gets up from a porch to get a drink requires no explanation.

The front porch wave is subtle. Done one way, and a perfect stranger will approach and sit down for a neighborly chat; done another, with a particular tilt of the head, and the same stranger keeps going, no offense taken. Our porch has taught me things I didn't know I was curious about. I sit gape-jawed many evenings, surprising myself with my rapt attention to a discussion about cloud formations Andy is having with people we barely know. I am learning about outcroppings and why they are very useful in creating barricades to prevent soil erosion, and that the biblical directive of resting soil in the seventh year is followed with good reason.

The neighborliness took me by surprise at first, but slowly, I began to shed my mask of self-imposed solitary confinement. Living in the city taught me to smile from afar and project a friendliness that could remain untested. Learning to be friendly up close, combined with the comfort of inviting chairs and cushions, has taught me that our porch is a version of a country social. Within days of our first summer in our home, I found myself keeping sweet tea in the fridge, hoping for a neighborly visit out front.

To me, porches also mean swings, and swings mean slowing life down for just a moment. When my girls were little, I used to stop at every playground we walked past and not only pushed my daughters on plastic swing seats, slung like the strap under a saddle, but also swung myself for a moment once the girls were satiated. I remember laughing out loud at how a simple swing could give me such a moment of mellow joy. So swaying, as if an invisible guest was rocking back and forth, our wooden porch swing beckons anyone to sit. Its comfortable pillows are covered in soft, thick bark cloth. This fabric has a texture of memory all its own, since it holds fast the original heritage of sodden tree bark, slapped and scraped roughly smooth in faraway lands. Today, cotton fabric manufacturers produce these same prints of loud but gentle patterns of foliage and fruits that were seen in so many 1930s and '40s kitchens across America. The faded prints are perfect for my porch, where relaxing is the only activity required.

There was a wonderful old barn several miles deeper into the country, where I would drive past herds of cows that piled on top of one another when it was particularly cold outside. I loved seeing this and imagined they were one huge family who loved each other very much. Their bland yet soulful faces held memories for me of innocent days long ago, when standing on a fence as a little girl would have kept me occupied for hours. This old barn had been turned into a little store, where I would occasionally go to forage for interesting objects. The barn owners had decided a long time ago that it would be a good idea to go through the countryside looking for abandoned objects on the side of the road to sell in their dirty barn for outrageous sums of money. It was my favorite place to shop.

I would drool over dilapidated chairs and light fixtures that didn't work at all. Andy refused to go with me ever since I made him carry a three-hundred-pound broken mirror to a cabinetmaker to fix the cracked frame, then to a decorative artist to repair the gold leaf, and then to a glassblower who specializes in antiques to have the back of the mirror resilvered. He said that my delight was directly related to his arm strength and that his back hurt just thinking about it.

I found something for the porch every time I visited. The last time I was there, I found an old watering can, which I carried home and then filled with hydrangeas cut from the yard. Arranging them inside my new find, I carried the can to the front porch, where it sat comfortably in its new home.

When our grown children come home to visit, they disappear from time to time, escaping to the front porch where conversations are gentler and quieter. Inside, at tables in the family room and dining room, louder conversations take place amid constant interruptions and a stream of activity: up, down, in, and out—little grandchildren underfoot, and the dog racing with a soft stuffed toy in his mouth, begging someone to play with him. The porch will have none of this.

Daughters sit on our swing and nestle their feet into their husbands' laps, closing their eyes with only the occasional murmur about the direction the breeze is blowing. The bark-cloth pillows are scrunched and crumpled, and the city seems far away.

Light

Light! more light! the shadows deepen,
And my life is ebbing low,
Throw the windows widely open:
Light! more light! before I go.
> —Francis Ellen Watkins Harper,
> "Let the Light Enter"

The stairs that led to our basement had a full-height door that blocked the entrance to the kitchen when opened. Beginning a descent to do laundry, there were just three short steps that ended in a small landing where you had to make a sharp left turn, carefully navigating a series of pipes and paraphernalia hanging low enough to hit your head. After multiple head bumps and bad words, I learned to duck. It was a treacherous journey to the washer and dryer, but oh, the dreams I had for this space. I longed to dig the floor down to create more height and design an office and cozy lower-level family room. An additional bedroom and a new bathroom were all part of the modifications I envisioned. I had no idea how long I would have to wait before one of these tasks could start though, as they each were so monumental. One day, as I headed to the catacombs carrying unpacked boxes, I became distracted by an idea that piqued my interest.

At the stair landing, another door led outside to a small red-brick patio. Here, an enormous walnut tree stood guard, spreading its branches much like wings and creating a magical, sun-speckled canopy. It was my favorite outdoor spot. I placed two small wrought-iron tables and chairs here, creating an intimate spot for dining or for anyone needing a bit of comfort, myself included. I still felt the occasional city twinge of homesickness, so finding ways to gentle my soul helped me slow my mind, allowing me to close my eyes for a moment and think about nothing.

Each day in the summer, Andy would go directly to this patio when he arrived home from work. He would take his man stance, ridding his mind of work thoughts as he gazed out toward the back. Eventually, satisfied with whatever man thoughts had been settled, Andy would fill a dish with fresh water from the hose, and Clyde would meander over, looking for love. Watching from the kitchen window, I saw this scene repeated countless times, and it never stopped making me happy.

Shortly after moving into our home and before the patio existed, a fit of organizational frenzy hit me. I began sorting through boxes I was bringing in from the carriage house. I had the kitchen door to the stairs open, as well as the door leading to the side yard, both doors solid and without windows. I was hauling boxes back and forth to the scruffy ground beyond the doors. Covered with mud and smelling like dank dust, I could tell that something was different about the stairs, the hallway, and the whole kitchen. There was brilliant light pouring in to redeem the day. I hollered to Andy and pointed toward the light as though we were trapped in a cave and I had discovered the way out. I explained my vision while he listened. This is something my husband does very well: He listens to me with a patience I had never experienced before meeting him.

On the other side of the stair-landing door was glorious light from the west, where colors from the sunset surprised me. This often-used but dark and lonely area of our home rarely saw natural light. The solution was to replace the original outside door with a new one that had glass in the top half, beveling to match the design of all the other exterior doors in our home. Creating a half-carriage door at the top of the stairs allowed light to flood into the central chase of our home. I imagined the house relieved, surprised, not aware of its dissatisfaction living in the dark. In changing these doors, we found inspiration for new kitchen plans, a redesign of the fireplace, the expansion of a beverage center for grown children visiting, and a new sitting area where we could enjoy the light splay onto the kitchen walls in red, gold, and bronze every evening. In the meandering pattern through the rooms on our main floor, now not one step in the circuitous journey is without natural light pouring in. We embrace the brilliance in the day, and we pleasure in the light of the moon at night.

We crave natural light and will seek it out in the darkness. Carefully designed artificial light is a fair substitute, but oh, there is nothing like natural light in the central rooms of a house where life is lived. A well-planned home makes use of natural light like water in a desert, doling it out as though it were liquid gold, measuring every drop. Artificial light has its uses. It can make me feel at home in my own house, since I can design purposeful task lighting where patterns of light illuminate my path as I go from room to room. I can create mood with dimmers and carefully place fixtures that provide personality and are unusual and fun. The point is to not neglect light, whether natural or artificial.

A room with poor lighting always seems a little sad and interrupted. Light can be very specific, and we see this in the importance of the well-placed lamp. Putting light precisely where I want it means that I can pick up a book and nestle into a cozy corner and start to read, when previously this dark spot would never have wooed me. Locating a pharmacy lamp, turning it on, and having light shine onto a page makes a little sitting area comfortable with nothing more than a flick of a switch.

The windows on the front of our house have glass that is beveled with thick leaded crystals cut into beautiful shapes. Since the front porch runs the full width of the house, covered with a broad roof, natural light can only reach this glass by making its way underneath the canopy, much like a wild animal peering through the brush. Southern light meanders artistically through the beveled glass windows, bringing the beauty of all the colors of the rainbow with it, throwing patterns of light over the floor and walls beyond. The stabs of light splay out onto the rugs and move from one side of the house to the other, creating warm patches that Clyde pays attention to throughout the day. He lies down first in the family room, where the morning light arcs out long and narrow, and then moves to the living room to rest in the afternoon sun as though home from a long journey. On cloudy days, Clyde sulks and retires to the kitchen door to wait for Andy to come home.

I wanted to bring beveled glass to the windows at the rear of our home. It just didn't seem fair that the windows at the back of the house were all nakedly plain when the view was so spectacular. The shaded seating area with an enormous maple tree that moved at the slightest breeze, the bounty of lilacs blooming purple and white but shy, and a giant fir that towered over the Hosta garden below, with stepping stones meandering a path from one side to the other, all deserved to be seen.

There was a small powder room nestled clumsily into a closet. A combination laundry room/pantry had a window looking out to the backyard. I couldn't see the sense of a window by the washing machine and the powder room in a closet, so I announced to Andy that I would like him to please move the laundry room to the basement, move the powder room to the pantry, and move the pantry to the present position of the closet. It was all very simple, just musical rooms in my mind's eye. I said this with optimistic enthusiasm while Andy stared at me for a moment with mouth firmly shut. Finally, he just said, "Are you serious?"

"Yes, of course, it will be fun!"

"My crazy wife who thinks everything can be done."

"It is a better design."

"Everything can always be worse. Everything can't always be better."

I would not be moved. "Sure, it can be worse, but if we can make it better, why not?"

"Because everything costs money."

I was undaunted by the eighteen-inch-thick granite foundation that would stubbornly refuse water pipes. I also knew that moving the washing machine and dryer to the basement would mean doing laundry in a dungeon for time incalculable, until we would decide to dynamite the entire basement and live in the land of mud for a year while digging out of the mess. I couldn't wait to start.

Walking into the renovated and newly located powder room months later, I relished with a clap of my hands the window of beveled glass made by my artisan hands. I watched as patterns of beautiful light sprayed colors onto the creamy walls of antique Rosselli wall covering. As I looked out the window, I saw our patio of original red brick, with moss growing between each old stone.

We still love to sit out here under the trees on summer evenings. Coming home from work, I find Andy in his usual spot on the patio. He frizzle-frazzles Clyde's head with his large, worn carpenter hands while he listens to my client escapades from the day. The light dims, and we go inside to watch the dark sky penetrate our windows and bring starry, starry night into our home.

The Kitchen

We owe much to the fruitful meditation of our sages, but a sane view of life is, after all, elaborated mainly in the kitchen.

  —Joseph Conrad, Preface to *A Handbook of Cookery for a Small House*

When we moved to the country, I had the romantic notion that I would begin to cook sumptuous meals immediately. I painted an image in my mind of pinching this and plucking that, much like what I saw on cooking shows. In the city, cooking was utilitarian for me, since food prepared in unique and amazing ways was so easily available at nearby restaurants. I liked to cook and could handle basic recipes, but I had never wandered far from the ordinary. I dreamed that I would begin to season with herbs harvested from my own garden and that I would become farm-to-table, my own table. What happened instead was the opening parlays of a feud: My kitchen and I did not get along. I talked to it rudely.

"You smug cooktop with your measly two burners. How are you are going to cook a dinner for twelve?" Changing out and upgrading this cooktop would be difficult in its present location, since it was installed in an awkward, angled peninsula with limited cabinetry below.

I quickly learned that I was going to have to live with cabinets and drawers that wouldn't open. Tugging, even gently, resulted in the sudden smack of a drawer front falling to the floor. Upper cabinet doors either were stuck firmly closed or swung open mysteriously on their own.

I can't count the number of times I accidentally bumped behinds with acquaintances while reaching for a glass in an upper cabinet. The ill-positioned peninsula, which started with a straight run and then suddenly turned at an odd angle, limited the use of the kitchen to no more than a single person. This countertop appendage should have been a model of efficiency but only allowed for eighteen inches of space on either side, so even gangly, thin children got in the way. The simple act of slicing up an apple was laborious, since it was interrupted every time anyone walked by. Move the chair in, let someone by, get up, close the refrigerator to allow the back door to open, close the oven to open the cabinet for pans, don't use the microwave if the dishwasher was being loaded—it was like a symphony in chaos. Kitchens are supposed to be the well-oiled machines of the home, and mine was the stalled car on the side of the road— abandoned and hopeless, with all the tires stripped off.

My earliest kitchen memories are with my mom, in a little house on the outskirts of Chicago. She would stack thick telephone books on top of a tubular metal chair that had a bright blue and white Naugahyde seat cushion. My mother would give me a small piece of dough, and I would roll it into a circle, patting it flat into starfish hands. She would show me how to tap cinnamon from the side of a tiny spoon and pinch sugar from a colorful bowl, letting each pinch of sweetness fall on top of the piecrust dough. Next came dropping dabs of butter, cut from a large chunk with the edge of a spoon, on top of the sugar and cinnamon. She taught me to rub butter on the bottom of a pan using a torn piece of waxed paper and how to keep my hands clean while cooking. I learned how to place my small concoction into the oven and wait impatiently for it to be done. Once baked and still warm, I would eat my little pie accompanied by a glass of milk. I was three years old, in a kitchen with hand-painted orange cabinets, and it was here my mom taught me how to cook.

My kitchen was designed for a cook employed by the owners of the house, who would have slept in a tiny room just outside the kitchen door. I see evidence of this small room by the marks on the ceiling that are still visible, though faded and worn. To make the kitchen larger, someone foraged space from this sleeping room, and now a table with chairs could fit. The problem was where to put the refrigerator. The location of choice appeared to be at a right angle to the back door, which did not allow anyone to enter easily. If Andy came in to get something, I had to leave the kitchen and step over to the table, unless I lifted myself up onto the counter so he could reach the sink.

I comforted myself with the knowledge that the new kitchen plans were sitting in a drawer near the beverage center. The beverage center had no beverages at all, let alone any cabinetry, but it was an idea shining in the future—and all good design starts that way. There would be a beverage center with coffee, tea, and cappuccinos beckoning to the sleepyhead sons-in-law as they walked in, scratching their arms and looking like little boys. They would come downstairs before their wives to see what I'd put out on the old farm table that sat proudly yet cramped in the middle of this tiny kitchen.

The table was too big for the space, but we forgave this and wrangled with it whenever the kids stayed with us. These early mornings were when the wild hoopla of having four daughters—each with a quiet husband who watched his wife live the hysteria that was, and still is, us—was gentled. I slid a large mug of hot coffee in front of each young man as he came down to the kitchen amid gentle hellos and the sound of chairs pulled out and in.

Gathering a tiny moment of peace to chat about life was precious indeed, a sacred time for Mother and "son" with open faces, open hearts, and asking, "What else do you need?" When a third and fourth person entered, the entire table had to be shoved to the side, and havoc ensued.

"How is your new job?" I asked one of our "sons" as he slid a chair back and sat down. I placed a mug of hot coffee in front of him. Reaching for the cream, he settled in for a conversation.

"Well, it's taking some getting used to, but . . ." A *blam* of interruption came with the scrape of the rustic barnwood table being dragged away from the windows by another "son," coming downstairs with sleepy eyes. This rearrangement meant the next newcomer wouldn't be able to reach the coffee pot, so I rose as calmly as I could, grabbed it from the counter, and placed it on the table.

"You were saying? Is it starting to get a bit more comfortable?"

A sudden bang of a chair had our coffee mugs jostling, spilling from those raised to lips. A daughter had entered the kitchen and attempted to sit down, but the table pulled out meant you couldn't get close to the sink, causing yet another collision.

"*Stop* moving the table. Let's all move it down a foot, reshuffle the chairs, and I'll get a new pot of courage started."

With this exclamation made by me, one of the boys left to go to the bathroom, another decided to take Clyde, who was nosing his way to the door, outside, and I was left alone to silently argue with my kitchen all by myself.

Making enough room for the refrigerator to open while daughters and their husbands were seated, or to pour coffee from what was *not* the beverage center, required vigilance and a hearty dose of determination. I remembered that most special moments in life are like this. They are carved out of random, unplanned acts. My kitchen could create these moments even when we were mad at each other.

The act of pouring a cup of coffee has always been ceremonial to me. Selecting a mug from the cabinet is still something I look forward to every day. Andy picks out a mug for me occasionally, loving these small moments of reaction he knows will come. He sets it out with a spoon, placed just so, and sometimes I use the one he selects. But on other days, he watches me from the table where he is reading the paper, peering over his glasses as I stand on the other side of the counter and inspect his selection, mulling it over. *I'm not sure. Maybe. No.* I open the cabinet door and stare for a full fifteen seconds before I pick the one I want and replace the one on the counter with this new choice. I pour hot black coffee into the mug and slide into a chair next to him, and he looks back down at his paper, smiling.

"In a mood today for red?" he asks without looking up.

"Yes, red. It is a red day," I respond. The safety I feel in Andy understanding my compulsions and accepting them as intimate truths makes me smile as I blow on my first cup of coffee, both hands clutched around my red cup.

Morning rituals often start in the kitchen, like the grind, scoop, and fill that our Cuisinart requires. Every night, I anticipate what tomorrow will bring by saying goodnight to our kitchen. I have always done this, no matter where I have lived. Even when my country kitchen and I were fighting, I tried to be respectful. Every night, I tuck it in, put away the dishes, and hang a fresh and colorful towel from the oven door. I make sure the sponges are neatly stacked one on top of the other and that the soap dispensers are full. I turn the banana bowl just so and make sure the peak of the yellow bananas contrasts nicely with the blue cobalt stripe that runs around the top edge of the creamy white ceramic bowl. The ledge above the sink, whose surface is made up of small one-inch-square French blue tiles, juts out awkwardly into the yard, but the window faces a magnificent maple tree that I look at dozens of times every day. I have filled this blue ledge with white pottery, and I make sure the blue tiles form a lovely circuitous path between the different shades of white bowls and pitchers. Dried baby's breath sits atop an old pitcher, and it is a white-on-white cloud against the sunset-sky glass behind it. Cutting boards rest against each other, relaxing until they are put to work again, and the strainer baskets are dry, waiting to be drenched with the first splash of cold water in the morning as the coffee pot is filled.

There is comfort in coffee, in salads, in baking, and in the quiet snapping of beans. A functional, well-designed kitchen heralds the arrival of absolutely everyone. Plan a party and set up every room with nestled coves of wonderful snacks and comfortable pillows beckoning for conversation, and they will look pristine when the party is over because everyone will be in the kitchen. Kitchens are places where people take off their masks, just as I do. I wear heels at work and flip-flops in the kitchen. I put my hair in a ponytail, and while I am cutting up a tomato, I listen to my daughters tell me their secrets as my granddaughter shouts out the ABCs. I sing at the top of my lungs to music on the radio, and Andy comes in to whirl me around the floor in a quick dance step spin. We feel young in our kitchen and comfortable with life, and anxieties spill out and feel better with a piece of refrigerator pizza or a cold piece of almost anything, especially if it is a vision of the familiar.

Our city kitchen was tiny, but it didn't bother me since it was laid out perfectly—like a small closet with perfect shelves and poles so that you could see everything and know what to wear on any given day. Open a cabinet door in any great kitchen layout and the contents are waiting to work. The forks wait, tines up, ready to pierce the nearest piece of food, and the baking pans are lined up at attention, ready for duty. In my Chicago kitchen I felt like Meryl Streep in the role of Julia Child, with wooden spoons clanging in rhythm against pots as if playing musical instruments. Reach for measuring cups, get water from the tap, grab ingredients from the refrigerator, stack plates on the table, whisk, stir, pour; this city kitchen worked in harmony with me, and it was fun to cook.

Our country kitchen was planned by the zoning committee of a government agency. It didn't work at all and expected to be paid and even appreciated.

I always smile when I see a scene in a movie where a gangster or a CEO of a publicly traded company has a particularly bad day and enters a large and well-designed kitchen late at night to sit in the dimly lit stage of worktable blues to eat a sandwich left for him in the refrigerator by some knowing chef. The scene depicts the only solace he will get, and the familiarity of having a snack in the middle of the night makes even the viewer feel better.

My country kitchen disappointed me, and that was a problem that was expensive to fix. There were numerous other mechanical issues, such as crushed sewer lines, which trumped my complaints about an awkward microwave placement. It wasn't long after we moved into our house that we discovered our kitchen was the bridge on the ship of all the mechanicals in our home. All the old knob-and-tube wiring, outdated and not to code even fifty years ago, led to the kitchen, where decades ago, a worker (not a certified electrician) took dozens of these cloth wires and decided in frustration to wind them up like Christmas lights taken down off a tree by someone infected with distemper. The cloth-covered wires were jumbled so that it was nearly impossible to know which wire led to which outlet. The only solution was to rip open half the walls and untangle wiring that was going to be discarded anyway.

I did not understand this and said so to Andy. He took on his familiar "I will explain this to you" stance and strode into the kitchen with his hands on his hips, pointing to the wiring like a man seeing the ocean for the first time. I listened for a few minutes, trying to understand his locution of why something must be redone first before you could rip it out and throw it away, but my eyes glazed over. When Andy put his arm down, I said, "I see." Satisfied, he left the room to find another nightmare somewhere else.

The plumbing pipes that ran through the kitchen walls burst one glorious day, and we had to rip open the remaining walls since it appeared the same worker (also not a plumber) decided to run all plumbing drains into a too-small drain, ensuring that it would all erupt in a wild deluge, in the middle of the day when we were not home. For years the sound of flushing toilets could be heard from the kitchen no matter which bathroom was used. Even when this was ultimately figured out, the walls remained open in the hopes that we would start the kitchen renovation next.

One day, in a spitfire storm of inspiration, I brought home a full fifty-yard bolt of chestnut-colored burlap. I cut lengths and stapled it to the kitchen walls, trapping and covering the large wall holes that exposed all manner of noxious black cast iron pipes. Since the outdoor sewer lines were still being worked on, Andy did not want to close the walls just yet. Not. Just. Yet.

On the burlap day in question, I wasn't going to look at the shiny large black pipes carrying sewage from the second floor to the main floor one more day, and so up went the burlap and down came my nervous apprehension. Since my expectations were often based on accomplishment, letting go of my need for completion was liberating. These large exposed pipes stared at me every day, reminding me of what was not yet done, and I needed to reframe my mind to seeing what was in progress.

It was as though a bright and shining light cracked open my countenance, and I was able to rest. Rest in the knowledge of potential instead of looking to complete something perfectly, fully, absolutely. I could learn to live with progress and let that be enough.

As I set up my ladder and began stapling, I let the burlap climb out onto the ceiling in a spurt of creative license that left Andy shouting from the basement that this was a waste of perfectly good staples.

"Those things cost money!" he shouted from a floor away.

"We're buying staples, not cabinets." Even as I flung these words back toward the stairs, I smiled. I had surprised myself with my awareness that I was enjoying a simple solution to a complex problem. I felt my shoulders relax as I reloaded my stapler.

The stapler I was using was a construction stapler, typically used to fasten waterproof liners onto the exterior of homes. You would slam it quickly and firmly against a wall, and staples would shoot out, securing the Tyvek, or in this case, chestnut-colored burlap. It was satisfying work. I hit the wall, stapling the burlap with all the strength my scrawny arms could muster. With each hit of the stapler against the wall, I was declaring my purpose in this kitchen. I was claiming it as mine. I stapled the burlap onto the walls as though building a rescue raft that would take me somewhere new.

With all its incongruities and points of nonfunctioning irritation, this kitchen belonged to me now, and it was here where I would mend the hearts of my family by serving up homemade soups and my mom's chocolate chip cookie recipe, always making time for one more cup of hot-brewed coffee, sipped while listening to the ones I love tell me about their day.

The Boys

*I'm not trouble at all. I'm just a guy trying to get a
girl to give him the time of day. I'm like every song on
the radio.*

—Hailey Abbott, Boy Crazy

It seems such a short time ago that I was pregnant with
Kimberly, my oldest daughter. I didn't care whether I had
a boy or a girl and was so excited that I wrote odes to
my unborn child. I wrote volumes in spiral notebooks,
espousing the virtues of unknown motherhood; the epistles
were love letters to both my baby and the world. I was
Mother Earth, and my baby was Simba, held up by Rafiki—
blessing not just our family but all of humankind. Then I
threw up violently for the next six months, and the vision
was replaced by the reality of shuffling around in a slightly
vomit-scented bathrobe.

Nine months after Kimberly was born, I was pregnant
with Kerianne, who graced our lives with huge, blue, knowing eyes and arms that wrapped around my neck. I bought a

double stroller so I could walk the streets of Chicago as the proudest mom in the world. Giving birth to Heather two years later gave Kimberly and Kerianne someone to fight over during playtime. Heather's spunk and smiling charm helped her hold her own, and Miranda came two years later to complete the set. Being the youngest, Mandy was the star the other girls doted on.

I insisted that my girls get along, remembering my mother and how she just expected us to be nice. Nice was not rewarded, it was expected, and I have come to admire the way she and my father parented with natural virtue and a sense of justice that did not come from books. It is true, though, that books were a huge part of their lives, and ours, but they were never referenced to teach potty training or how to raise a good little boy or girl. My parents' instructions on parenting came from the gut, and everyone seemed to know the rules. I expected my daughters to be good and work hard, and developing sisterly loyalty rounded out the simple list of my child-raising declarations. These became the core elements of their growing-up years. I also had no time to imagine anything different, since four girls in six years took all my time.

Hair was a major part of our lives, and the morning lineup consisted of being called into the dining room, one at a time, where I had laid plastic bins filled with all the accoutrements necessary for long hair with braids, ponytails, and buns. Little girls with long tresses, two blond and two brunettes, made for tangles and snarls that had to be tamed to make it through a day of school and the events that followed. Swim lessons meant washing chlorine out of their hair every day and then tightly winding their hair into buns for ballet and gymnastics later in the afternoon. Brushing out long tresses at night just to start the whole thing over again in the morning often had me feeling like the owner of a hair salon. In between sports, hairstyles and moods changed quickly; where long tresses with head-bands were fine a day before, suddenly French braids were requested on a moment's notice. I began to set term limits to styles.

Baubles and beads and barrettes and bracelets were mixed in with swim caps, ballet slippers, leotards, and tennis racquets. Our back porch mudroom walls were lined with snowsuits in bright pink and lavender for sledding and ice-skating. Long scarves and colorful mittens, adorned with pictures of ponies, imps, and elves, were stored in metal milk crates painted green, each one hanging from large silver hooks. Below the crates were neat rows of bright red wooden clogs, worn by each girl year after year. Growing out of one pair meant slipping into another, and when the last little foot graced the last Swedish clog, it meant the girls were growing up.

And then came the boys.

One by one, these testosterone-laced young guys crossed our threshold.

When the girls went to college, Andy and I wondered whom they might meet. Would they meet good men? Valiant, courageous men who would put themselves last and our daughters first? Brave men who would face trials calmly and lead with vision? Life partners who would complement our girls, enriching their lives in the process? The mainstay word we added to our vocabulary during these years was: *eventually*.

Eventually, we met Nick, our first son-in-law. We still tell their love story over the dining room table, starting with Nick wondering how to approach Heather at Great America, an amusement park north of Chicago. Landing on an offer of cheese fries seemed appropriate, and well, it worked! When Kerianne met Ken, we were offered tidbits, more than details, about the "guy in the white truck" she had seen at church. "Tell tell tell!" became our squeals. Kimberly and Jeremy also met at church. Jeremy described how smitten he was just watching Kimberly interact with others. Patrick and Mandy's love story began with rock climbing.

Our reactions leapfrogged from skepticism to surprise, and then to delight. For each of our girls, dating led to an engagement, and then to a wedding ceremony, the fourth one representative of how our lives would be different.

The wedding of our youngest daughter, Miranda, really was magical. Pretty bridesmaids in fancy dresses held tiny green rosebud-lidded boxes. We all waited for the kiss. Then the bridesmaids, balancing on heels, lifted the lids on cue, and the butterflies fluttered to freedom, providing a living veil. Miranda, our last little girl, said her vows and joined the ranks of her three married sisters. How perfect that butterflies lifting into the sky in a fluttery, disorganized, and lovely dance should forever symbolize, in my mind, the boys who changed the feminine mystique that had held our home captive for three decades. The first boy entered our outrageously girlish lives seven years earlier. Nick saw the sparkle in Heather's eyes and grasped the glorious fire-cracker charm of her soul, and that was that!

These young men have changed everything. It is not just the shoes or the bathroom time, or even the vacant stares or preoccupation with sports. We have experienced changes to the number of towels in the laundry, and bed linens are crumpled into wild balls of chaos every morning. The biggest change, though, is food consumption. The pantry is completely different. What was once a well-stocked room, filled with the scent of a savory spice shop and shelves lined with staples of quinoa, oats, and soups, now possesses the look of a shop soon going out of business—shelves empty and forlorn. With visits on most of our weekends, and often mid-week stop-ins as well, we never have leftovers anymore. The days of chili that tastes better the second day are gone forever.

I have three brothers, and when I was a child, my mother labeled items in the refrigerator. I have now formed a new respect for this system and am tempted to copycat her idea. It was not a system that named foods. The signs read more like NOT FOR YOU, or DO NOT EAT, or I CAN SEE YOU. While I was growing up, the only foods in our refrigerator that didn't have a warning label were the condiments.

In my childhood years, we always had food and lots of it, but my brothers were known to consume whole pot roasts intended for our family's evening dinner. Without proper labeling, I don't think any families with young boys would eat. The parents and the girls would eat cereal—wait, no— even that is not safe. The boys eat their morning cereal by carrying the box to the table with a carton of milk. They fill their bowl with cereal, pour the milk, and consume the bowl of cereal. This is repeated until the box is empty. Leaving the house meant the food was gone. Boys brought a new pattern to eating in our home, and having food around that can be eaten standing up is now my priority when selecting recipes. In fact, I must plan for sitting-down food and standing-up food, and then all the food in between.

I take inspiration from my mom. She would make an enormous pot of spaghetti sauce and dole out small "schnitzels," as she liked to call them, when we came home from school starving and unable to wait until dinner. Cooking a small amount of "after-school pasta" to be eaten standing up, with sauce made early enough to stave off our hunger pains before dinner, is something I am now doing regularly.

Lately, our television remotes have become undecipherable because of the boys, and impossible configurations of channel-switches have left us watching just three channels when 787 are available. Andy can talk to these young men gracing our lives about electronics, but they speak a language of orbs and dashes and cabling wires that sound very important. I try to follow but get lost when they reach the tenth decibel configuration of fiber optic cables from the North. I tried to join the conversation once by saying, "What?" The next thirty minutes were filled with words they made up, though their faces were very serious, and I nodded often to make them feel better. When they were done with answering my question, they were hungry, and I was exhausted. Since we had only breadcrumbs in the drawer, I called the pizza delivery man.

The timbre of boys' voices is different from girls'. The low rumble heard when the boys are talking is a stark contrast to the sounds coming from the girls' direction. The girls talk loudly, with pitches that range continually from high to low. Punctuations of laughter and shrieks of exclamation create constant interruptions in their conversation. The girls' voices are fast-paced and quick quick, and if you don't keep up, you're out, moved past, on to the next topic. Nobody seems to mind, as the conversation winds back around again like a tapestry in song. It is precisely this kind of conversation that I am used to. Jump rope double Dutch conversation: Watch for a second, get your timing, and then leap in and join the harmonic chaos. A newcomer watches, jumps in, and is sent flying with tangled legs to the side of the conversation—but encouraged to try again. Warmth and laughter are the norm, and sometimes the boys give up, nestling into their own world of man talk. The girls ask the boys to come and join them, and sometimes they do, but sometimes they mimic Andy's words when he says to me, "I just like to watch you live."

Accommodating a growing population of men has meant making changes to our home remodel plans. We are thrilled to have our lives graced with the girls bringing their guys over often and continually, including the continual run to the grocery store as baseline, and we have added comfy seating in every room, since conversations are caught more than prompted. Blooming from the coupling all around us is an expanded knowledge of almost every topic, and this enriches us every time we are all together. Where one young man knows about trucks, another has explored American history. From whether a leak under a car engine is serious to which president was responsible for our highway system, we have it covered. Andy does mourn the lack of a plumber in the family, one of his suggestions when the girls began dating that was never heeded.

Other, more subtle changes are evident: larger stacks of towels, "man soap" (as Andy calls it), crock-pot creations, more boisterous game nights, and movie lists that include the names of planets and machines. Large shoes are left under coffee tables; newspapers are in all the bathrooms. Every Friday night, we listen for the back door to open, and we holler to the girls and their boys to come on in.

Sounds

In every sound, the hidden silence sleeps.
            —Dejan Stojanovic

Outside our bedroom window was a beautiful magnolia tree. Its blossoms were nearly hysterical in their pink bursts of color. This should have meant enjoyable morning viewings during the early spring of our first year in our Woodstock home, but country sounds kept me up at night. Open windows and the soft breezes I had romanticized brought with them the unanticipated sounds of owls hooting, bats careening through the sky accompanied by screeches, and various other unseen scramblings of imagined wild animals. I would get up to see what was going on, peer into the yard only to see red eyes staring back at me, prompting a run-and-dive back to bed. My sleep was constantly interrupted by this new nighttime ritual.

One morning, I woke up irritated by the sound of birds chirping. I had hoped to sleep in, but birds began to sing outside our bedroom windows with such a cheerful vengeance that I questioned their motives.

"Darn birds!" I said out loud.

Andy laughed into his pillow and told me that I was back-sliding in my country-living progress. Birds, he informed me, were part of the country experience, and he loved to wake to the sounds of their chuffed song. I lay very still and listened. I had to admit that their cheerfulness did make me feel like I was in a Disney film. I was determined to do better, since I felt more like the evil stepmother than Cinderella, who had darling birds help her dress. In contrast to the optimism all around me, I pulled the sheets up over my head and stewed.

As I ruminated under the covers, I remembered the constant nature of city sounds. It was silence that made me sit up in the middle of the night in Chicago.

"What is that? Did you hear that?" I jostled my husband awake beside me.

"I didn't hear anything."

"Exactly! Go check."

Silence in the city means sneaking around, doing things furtively and suspiciously. Sounds are so mixed and varied that the hum of incessant noise is a comfort and solace. I used to wake up suddenly at 4 a.m. when the neighbor's music stopped. My reaction to the sounds of the country was similar to how I felt about driving down long country roads with no streetlights every hundred feet. I felt that danger lurked in the middle of every cornfield, that farmhouses nestled into the countryside were possible havens of torture. Mice scurrying about acres away from any house left the girls and me screaming and running for the nearest picnic table, leaping up with shrieks shrill enough to cause usually calm dairy cows to stampede.

I had to admit, though, I did love the country sheep. I was smitten with the skinny and scrawny sheep that looked like they had been zipped out of their winter coats and left to shiver outdoors, embarrassingly naked. Seeing those same sheep six months later, looking like round bales of enormous hay from afar, only to have black eyes peer out at me from the roundness as I approached, tugged at me. Little by little, I began to revamp my thinking. It seemed to me that everything in the country had a purpose and was working toward a common goal of harmony. There was a collaboration of sorts between the animals feeding on the grain that grew in the field beside them and the humans in the houses taking care of the animals, and the wheel went round and round. I have a need for completion, which is a trait that lends itself nicely to my field of design. I push hard toward the end of the circle of a project, and I was seeing this same characteristic in the farmlands surrounding me. The bleat and the swish and the rumble of farm equipment formed a unique musical cadence I had not heard before.

Listening to the birds on that Saturday morning showed me more than my annoyance. Could I allow the chirps to penetrate my frenetic soul? That same morning, I made coffee as usual, mulling over the sounds I was creating. *Scoop, scratch, splash, pour, scrape,* all comforting in their ordinariness. I renewed my commitment to country living and dressed for my weekend ritual at the farmers market. I wandered from fresh vegetable stands to fruit displays, noticing the murmur of conversation. Price haggling could be heard with the high and low punctuation points as deals were struck. Wheels on carts and wagons scraped over cobblestone, creating a *braaaap* sound as background noise, and the clump of cowboy boots was the drumbeat cadence grounding it all.

Returning home, armed with the knowledge that the tassels on corn are very important, I made blueberry pancakes with my haul from the morning trek to the square. The circular scrape of spoon against earthenware, and the accompanying plop into the pan with the sizzle before the flip, were sounds of comfort and hominess.

Purposeful in my self-renovation, I began developing new habits that grounded me. I took my first cup of hot coffee and stood in the living room, looking out the window to the yard beyond. I listened to the sounds of the house. I liked to wake up my house by rising early and having a moment to gather my thoughts before the tyranny of the urgent took over my mind. Get up, let dog out, make coffee, let dog in, pour coffee, and stand, letting the day's beginning soak into me.

Mug in hand, I would meander from room to room, gently waking up each room as I went. I walked into the family room, where pillows lined the back and corners of the much-used sofa. As I shook each pillow awake, I heard Andy's voice in my mind, and I looked forward to evening, even though it was the crack of dawn. I knew that later that evening, sitting on this very sofa, I would listen to him talk to me about wood and pneumatic nailers and why groundwater in Northern Illinois has no place to go. Down forms were zipped inside the pillows and allowed us to scrunch our arms into them when we snuggled in at the end of a long day. These pillows always ended up jumbled and loved every day.

I would hear Clyde jingle his way toward me, following me as I performed my morning rituals. His collar and tags made a musical sound as he padded along—then, a sudden clump to the floor if I took too long. I listened as the school buses went down South Street. Since our four-square sits atop a hill, every truck or bus that passes must gun their engines just a little bit to make the ascent. This same pattern is repeated later when the school day is over. There is a consistent motorized hum that tells me what time of day it is. I could set my morning and afternoon clock by the sound of the Blue Bird School Bus Company.

Soon after the buses, I hear high school girls and boys, and I know that I must let Clyde onto the front porch. He stretches his legs out in front of him, bending them at the knee joint, hanging his paws over the front step contentedly.

Ordinary days move from sound to sound in our house, and the predictable pattern is comforting. Subtle changes tell me that time is passing and that seasons are changing. Wind blowing through a tree laden with leaves sounds different than through a winter tree, where the howling is crisper, lonelier. Just as nature produces sounds of transition, so do weekends.

Saturdays are workdays around the house, and I love these roll-up-your-sleeves-and-tackle-the-project-at-hand days. There is something about a Saturday that begets scrubbing, wrestling with an angry garden of thorns, and mucking about outside with a rake. On Saturdays, I remember my dad. As a young girl, I woke up on Saturdays to the sound of my father coming into our bedrooms, putting up the shades, and singing, "It's a beautiful day!" at the top of his lungs. My Dad worked on Saturdays doing the books for a golf club nearby; as an accountant, providing for a family of six children meant that having more than one day off a week was a luxury he could not afford. But Saturdays were fun even for him, and he got an enormous kick out of waking up sleepyhead children and putting us to work. He would write out a list and put it on the refrigerator with chores for the boys and chores for the girls, and since there were three of each, it was pretty much fair.

My parents had this part worked out ever since we argued about whose bowl of ice cream was bigger, and my mother announced that she had weighed them. Peering into our ice cream bowls and giving sidelong glances to each other, my brothers, sisters, and I didn't know how to respond to this logic, so we accepted it then and there that our parents could be trusted to dole out portions of goodness equitably. The last thing my dad would say on a Saturday morning before heading out the door was, "Help your mother." And so, we did, and a clatter of sound ensued as six tumbling children ran to the kitchen to see what was on the list.

My brothers would start hosing down the back patio, basically making a mess, while I was inside the green station wagon, scrubbing the seats with my sister Jenny. I was in the front, and she was in the back. We would make faces at my brothers as they aimed water at the outside of the car. Smearing dirt, muddy puddles, water everywhere—I don't know how my mother could stand it. I suppose she got a few minutes of peace inside the house, with the four big kids outside creating havoc.

I can still hear my father's sing-song voice when I close my eyes. This has set the tone for my worldview on mornings, and I know it comes from parents who were thoughtful in their approach to child-rearing. This was a time when everyone had lots of kids, and neighborhoods at night had foraging groups of young children running around, playing kick the can, waiting for the sound of a dad whistling through his teeth to tell them it was time to come home. I take the memories of my parents, who have been gone a long time, and nestle them on the most precious shelves of my mind's memory closet. I close the door reverently until next time.

Arranging sounds in a home is akin to arranging furniture. Just as a traffic pattern can direct the flow of people easily from one place to the next, sound is part of the process of elevating the comfort level in the places we live. There is a sound of activity that follows as we walk through our homes, whether it be the soft sound of socks on the floor from a rumpled, sweatpants-clad late riser, or the crisp clack-clack of heels on the same floor when hurriedly leaving for work. Our minds react to these sounds with the anticipation of the activity each sound brings.

When the girls come over, I can tell who enters, even if I'm on a different floor, by the sound of the footsteps. When all the kids come over, I think about the sounds as much as I think about the food. The initial hubbub and banter need to be centered, like the hub of a large and well-functioning wheel. We want to be near and pulled toward each other by the sounds of our hugs and kisses and greetings. It is a centrifugal force of love, and reveling in its power matters to each member of the family. We are here, and this is now.

The sounds of family disperse through the house and permeate the walls. These sounds become trapped in our memories. We want to discover them at hidden moments of wonder, coming across them like a dazzling piece of bright glass in the sand, and oh!

One afternoon, I sat at the kitchen table with Kimberly. She quietly talked to me as she nursed. Heather joined us, with my newest grandchild sleeping sweetly in her arms. We smiled at the sounds of a feeding baby relishing mother's milk, where all the comfort and joy an infant can muster is evident in a small, sweet hand clutching Mommy's breast. We reveled in the gentle sounds of a sleeping infant, so secure, so peaceful, so innocent.

One room away in the dining room, Kerianne and Miranda set the table for dinner that night. The "red card box" was prominently set out at my place, to be passed around and cards pulled, cajoling us into riotous conversation about topics such as what we would do with a million dollars if we had it to spend in a single day. The sound of wine glasses chinking as they were taken out of the butler's pantry cabinets were muffled by the walls separating the kitchen from the dining room, but they made a pretty soprano note, like a bell randomly struck. The low notes of men talking were heard from the family room. The topic appeared to be automotive, which was confirmed later as Andy, Ken, Jeremy, Patrick, and Nick all piled out the door to go to the nearest dealership to look at pickup trucks. From the lower level, we heard the clatter of dominoes splaying out on the wood floor as Summer, our two-year-old granddaughter, poured out a metal box of delight.

All these sounds are distinct and separate, and yet they provide a symphony of family tradition. In arranging rooms, I am arranging dreams and giving a place and purpose for everyone to bring their own harmony to the mixture of instruments. Where one sound is loud and boisterous, another enters with the melodious voice of baby comfort, cooing, while yet another pierces the silence with giggles and laughter, or the gentle whispers of a conversation. Andy and I dreamed of this when we bought this old house. I remember standing out front the first time we saw it. Silent, and listening. We were listening to a mental picture we were painting, listening to the story we were telling ourselves. A vision, really, of friends and family gathered.

Now we stand and listen to the sounds of family on every floor, coming from every room. I am comforted by the thought that nothing can drown out the sounds of bare feet on wood floors in an old house that is ours.

Details

To create something exceptional, your mindset must be relentlessly focused on the smallest detail.

—Giorgio Armani

I love the combination of harmony and contrast that details can create in a space. See that carved corbel at the hallway ceiling, made of old pinewood that is split and worn? At first glance, it feels random, but it leads our eye to the aged wood beam above the fireplace, held up with large iron bolts. The dull surface of the iron contrasts with the sheen of the bronzed glass mirror hung above the mantel, and the mirror reflects the iron chandelier, bringing the circular route of our gaze to completion. We may not realize that our eye registers each item or even understand the circuitous path it has taken, but we feel satisfied, even if we don't know why. These are the elements that make a space memorable and comfortable. Our mind sighs in satisfaction, which is why one can sit and wait patiently in some lobbies but feel unease in others. Often, our mood plays a role, but the furnishings and surroundings have been carefully curated for our comfort. I believe the same care should be taken when appointing the interior of a home.

I love old houses with their meandering rooms, as though the house forgot where it was going. Hidden sliding doors and staircases with interesting balusters make every step a project in observation. Running my hands over newel posts carved to look like the head of a falcon, I wonder about the decision to make it a falcon and not a panther or a bear. I love the search for interesting objects and furniture for clients.

"Barbara, I found two perfect chairs for your den. The upholstered arms end in carved lion heads. They look ratty now, but once we put in new springs, new ties, new fills, new fabrics, and touch up all the stains, you will love them."

"Well, you have found some amazing things that we are still enjoying, so go ahead."

And go ahead I did, and now when these clients sit in the den, sinking into down cushions as their forearms nestle into soft velvet upholstery, their hands curl around the heads of old lions who have held up many a hand over the last hundred years. There is a special satisfaction that comes from renovating something that others have loved and used for decade upon decade. We connect with people we've never met, and we experience, perhaps, the same comfort.

I have slid open a thick slab of heavy pocket door to discover shelves, ceiling to floor, holding artifacts from trips abroad—dusty and worn, yet precious and loved. In one old home, I discovered a passageway through a closet into an anteroom, long ago used for reading and reflection. What were they reading, and why so secretive? I ponder these questions and smile as I think about the decision made and the directive given.

"Yes, hide that room and don't tell anyone," I imagine someone saying to a builder in the late 1800s. I would love to have a secret room. I have many in my mind. I store thoughts that I cannot communicate, like my need for approval, and the way I am embarrassed to admit that I hate my Roman nose. If I had a secret room, I would go, sit there, and read about other Romans and how they overcame the stigma. I would fit it out with stacks of books acting like end tables, and I would need a sofa, not a chair, since I do like to eventually close my eyes and stretch out. My secret room would tell the stories of my writing endeavors: old publications of op-ed pieces filled with rantings about things that no longer seem important. Sketches and paintings from when I was an artist would line the walls. I would put my remembrances of my mother in that room—the way she had of making me believe in family, even when it was hard.

My mom once told me of a closet she had as a little girl, where she would go after finishing her chores and while waiting for her mother and father to come home from work. Filled with comic books and some sort of small treat, she retreated there every day, settling her own crowded mind and determining to be good. I am much like my mother, so my secret room would ultimately be the place where I could go to miss her.

Once, at a client's project out of state, when opening a wall to redo the electrical wiring, we found large windows buried and covered up rather than removed. Why? What could no longer bear to be seen?

"Darling, if I have to look at those neighbors one more time, I'll scream."

"Sweetheart, they are five acres away, and you can't possibly see them from these windows."

"Well, I know they are there and they stole our cow at the auction."

"They didn't steal it—they bought it fair and square."

"Well, it was a steal no matter what you say. Get rid of these windows—I can't bear to look out of them."

This is the sort of imagined conversation I laugh about, wondering about Dotty or Fred or Myrtle, and everything just becoming too much, until up went the wood lath and down went the view.

I have worked for the owners of an old estate in Indiana, rumored to be a getaway spot for Al Capone. It possessed multiple entrances and exits, and I delight at the instructions that must have been given to produce this result. In another time and place, while designing a revised interior for a lovely older arts and crafts home, I was instructed by a client to create a below-ground walk-in safe room using Dillinger's jail cell door as the entrance. Oh, the joy of creative interiors using unusual found objects! It is these sorts of details that create depth in an otherwise ordinary house. I love to take a found object and incorporate it into a new design. Ways to breathe fresh air into a home include: using old knobs from the home of a loved one, restoring old plaster rather than removing it, burnishing hardware to a new luster, or replacing floorboards in a random pattern to showcase warm, rich-toned wood that has been hand-waxed and shimmers.

Inspiration often begets inspiration, and so it is easy to see how an artisan could move from one detail to another, bringing a home to life with wood, brick, and stone. A tapestry of intricacy begins to unfold as triple-layer crown molding leads to a tall base in two pieces, with rich Venetian plaster between the top of one and the bottom of the other. These details caress the interior of a house, making it personal. An intimacy develops between the occupant and the domain itself. It is this harmony, this partnership, that I longed to bring to our house on a hill.

"Why are you asking me to insert this old metal ring into the top of this beam?" was the sort of question Andy used to ask me.

After years of witnessing me capping columns with hammered copper, mortising old printed boards into floors, hanging barn doors harvested from buildings, foraging for hardware in abandoned warehouses, installing recessed shelves made from found and flat pieces of stone, and taking aging crates apart to use as wall art, he has learned to go with it. The result is always something everyone is proud of, and conversations about these details bloom like wild roses.

The first time I entered our country home, I noticed gorgeous fretwork in one very specific area of the main floor. There was a small separation in the living room, where a rectangular space declared its importance by its proximity to the large leaded-glass window at the front of the house. A carved pair of corbels, high at the ceiling, were hard for the eye to resist. Narrow vertical panels descended from the corbels, each possessing different hand-carved floral designs. The cutout patterns allowed light from the window to penetrate the room. Centered between these panels, which ran from ceiling to floor, was the entrance into this cozy area.

I needed to understand the significance. Why the intricate carvings here? Was this common to all homes built to replicate English Victorians at the turn of the nineteenth century in America? My research led me to discover that these decorative areas in homestead houses, built by people of affluence at the time, were basically the size of a casket, with just enough room added for a pathway around it for viewing. This special area allowed visitors to come and pay their respects to the family of the deceased.

Our home had been built for a person of consequence—someone who could afford a large piece of property and position a house proudly atop a hill only a few short blocks from the town square. This house had been designed with all the bells and whistles the era dictated. Births, deaths, and the cadence of life went on here for many generations. As friends and loved ones came for a funeral viewing, the deceased had a place of honor right off the main parlor, while the adjoining rooms provided ample space to receive mourners and well-wishers.

I found this respectful, and although I did want to pay homage to the history of this house, under no circumstances was I going to have a death-viewing camp set up in my home. I could think of a much better way to use this space.

Since books have been a companion my entire life, an idea simmered. Even before I could read, at the age of three, I was pouring over the blue *My Book House* collection and making up stories to go along with the pictures, knowing the undecipherable words meant something magical. My mind was a pool of gibberish, and I often felt restless and nervous as my thoughts raced unbidden. I found in my early formative years that opening a book calmed me down. Turning a page was deliberate, organized, steady. It went from point A to point B, each page, one after the other, and on and on. This showcased a pattern I could follow, a way to put my mind away for the night.

This living room alcove, once set aside for death, would become a place of comfort and renewal for me—a place for conversation, reading, and renewal. Even though it is an alcove with no door, it is a special area. The fretwork has been removed, while the corbels remain, reminding me of the care and detail this house has always possessed. Matching loveseats placed across from one another provide a comfortable spot when I'm alone, and a perfect conversation nook when family and friends join me here. The windows, where the glass ripples from being poured onto sand when formed, are reflections of beautiful scenes showcasing the porch and hydrangea beyond. A rectangular table sits between the small sofas, laden with stacks of books.

If I want to doze between chapters, I can just fit on one of the loveseats, reclining sideways with my knees dangling over one of its arms. I pick up a book from the piles before me, and my world returns to a place only a book can take me.

My grandchildren climb into my lap, handing me a book of their choosing. We cuddle up and travel together, exploring new worlds with every page we turn. I sigh as calm descends, inside and out.

The Wood Beneath Our Feet

*Why don't we go back to wood racquets? Then we
would see the best tennis played.*

—John McEnroe

Stepping with bare feet onto an old wood floor feels
natural, as though it is something our feet have been
looking for all their lives. Smooth not for the sanding, but
for the many years of walking, scuffing, trotting, stumbling,
living. Much like old stone steps worn smooth and center
swayed, nothing can quite mimic this polished feel, and our
feet know it. Just like I know that the worn-out elements of
my frenetic soul are smoothing into something better than
when they started: softer, gentler, nicer, and less reactionary.

Often, when something unplanned would happen, my
first thoughts led to suspicion. Even if it was innocent, like
an invitation, I wondered if it would disrupt a self-imposed
structure of harmony. I used to try and see ways I could say
no before I would say yes. I have been invited to things I
would love to do, and the first thing that popped into my

mind was fear. I was afraid to go. "What if I do something wrong? I might embarrass myself," was my first reaction to most invitations in my earlier years.

To counter this, I have been learning to lean into the building blocks of my life and allow the human experience of wonder and joy to invade my decision-making. I don't want to close myself off to the multitude of blessings that can come from human interaction. Little by little, I am less worried about what I might say or do and have become open to the imperfect.

"I would love to go. Let me get my coat," I replied to a friend's sudden invitation to grab a cup of coffee at the new restaurant in town. We sat for nearly two hours, connecting over commonalities and eventually sharing some struggles that had us looking into each other's eyes and finding empathy and understanding. I would have missed this had I stuck to my old ways.

"Come on in—I'll make some fresh coffee," I said to a neighbor stopping by unexpectedly when I literally had nothing to do but hide away. I invited her in, and our conversation meandered its way to apple orchards in the area, where I proceeded to learn about pruning—something two of our trees desperately needed. Exchanging information, we promised to do this again, and I found myself looking forward to the prospect. After she left, I went outside and stared at our trees for a long time.

Suddenly, upon reflection, I find myself becoming the person I have always wanted to be: open, kind, welcoming, less judgmental and frightened, and more spontaneous.

I come from a long line of overreactors who expand easily into laughter, sobs, frightful yelps, or tight embraces. Rarely do we consider first what we are feeling; we just go with it. I haven't seen you for a long time? Watch out for the full-arm hug wrap. A funny scene in a movie? Only a belly laugh will do. The last chapter of *Les Misérables*? Crumpled in my place. Easily startled by my husband walking up behind me innocently, I scream. Every time.

"Who did you think it was?" Andy asks boyishly.

Every year, on the first day it snows, Andy likes to do a donut with his truck, slamming on the brakes and seeing how it holds on the ice. My screams are part of the experience now, along with the requirement of an open parking lot with nothing in our way. We always end up laughing, even though my first responses were more like muffled tears.

For every overreaction on my part, Andy is a point of calm consideration. I envy his even keel. It is exhausting to have my emotions so raw and exposed all the time. It is as though all the events in a day pile up and land on my reflexes and, ultimately, my nerves. My anxiety is a low simmer that is always there in the background. The flame might go higher at times, but mostly it exists as a dim light at the back of my eyes. I might do something wrong. I could possibly disappoint someone. A project might go so badly that we lose money and not even break even. I don't know what I'm doing. Help!

Learning to calm down, an elusive-enough goal to cause me to search in the brambles of daily living, has been a lifelong effort. Stepping out of bed onto an old, knotty pinewood floor, warm and silky smooth from over one hundred years of use, I breathe out a small, soulful sigh of appreciation.

I did not walk on wood floors when I was growing up. My parents' first home was a house built on a slab of concrete, and the floors were covered in eight-by-eight-inch brittle tiles that were most certainly installed with an adhesive containing asbestos. When my mother decided she was tired of this floor, covering the original was easier, and ultimately safer, though safety was definitely not considered at the time.

My mom was a young woman with many young children, determined to have a continual project in the pipeline. These do-it-yourself projects were never quite completed with skill, but if energy could be bottled, her cap would have blown off due to the pressure of grit and desire inside.

Peel-and-stick tiles were purchased wherever it would have been the least expensive, and the method of installation was zip-zip, get it done. If something did not line up, oh well. This resulted in many childhood years of tiles popping off, sliding around, with corners chipped and missing. But my mother, an eternal optimist when it came to home renovations, was happy with the results. I was happy too because her happiness invaded me at a molecular level.

As a child, I ran from the kitchen to the living room with feet bare, hopscotching my way across the pattern the tiles made for me. Leading me through space, this also gave a boundary to my happiness. I liked emotions in neat and tidy groupings, since I had so many of them openly displayed.

"I can't go to school! My socks are not high enough! I can't go!"

"Maidy, yes you can, and you will. Change socks, and your brothers will wait."

Whether it was a ponytail not positioned properly on my head or socks that wouldn't obey, everything was a crisis. Through my grammar school days, I learned to memorize what could be considered reasonable: "Mommy, Jimbo's eyes are loose but not out," or the unreasonable: "My bed don't got no underneath," I said in distress about my top bunk. Not everything required crisis management, and I eventually learned to calm down outwardly, hiding my true nature. I sorted through possible topics of anxiety and learned that a lot can happen in a day, and I didn't have to spin at high speed every moment. This began my mind's journey into self-reflection, a place I must visit every day even now, to balance my discomposure with the serene.

I thought that everyone who lived in houses with wood floors was rich. My mother cleaned a few nearby homes for extra cash, and several times I went with her. I would help in a somewhat haphazard manner, shuffling a dusting cloth across furniture I had never seen before. Fancy dining rooms, high ceilings, opulent draperies, all memorable to my young eyes, but it was the floors that grabbed my attention. Wood floors in badeous colors of reddish and rich brown, and since we would take off our shoes to clean, I could stand and let my bare feet take in the warmth. This background, spread out for all the furniture to sit on, was perfect to my youthful eyes. Like looking into the eyes of a calm horse, allowing me to stroke its muscled neck, these wood floors felt powerful and lustrous.

Sounds were different on wood floors, too. The clatter of every toy, chair, or shoe in our home reverberated into other rooms, but these wood floors, in muted colors of the earth, softened even the sounds of living.

Ever since, wood floors call to me to calm down, to let out a sigh, to gentle my soul, to be home. Varied and complicated, evident in raw form for all to see, yet fabricated into a beautiful warmth that is useful, long-lasting, and full of irregularities. I have a kindred connection to what is below my feet.

There are varying species of wood floors in our lovely old house, and I appreciate them all. From walnut to red oak to knotty pine to V-cut maple, they all speak to the care and planning of the original homestead owner. There is a patterned border of inlaid walnut around the living room floor, where the center and edges are thin-cut red oak that has been worn to a natural sheen. Smack dab at the bottom of the stairs is a large, old iron grate that you must step on every time you go up or down. This floor grill covered the only warm air supply in the large living room. Coupled with the complete lack of insulation, this system was inefficient at best and freezing at worst. Two years into our occupation, we changed out a large, antiquated and inefficient furnace for a new system of heating and cooling, where this grate would no longer be necessary. It cut directly into the lovely border of walnut carvings at the floor's edge and required an artisan to fill in the pattern once the grate was removed.

Kevin, a wood flooring specialist, came in our front door, and when I showed him what needed to be done, he got down on one knee and ran large hands over the floor lovingly. He scuffled around, peering at corner cuts, and I left him to his examination. When he was done, he came and found me in the kitchen.

"Well, she is old, but I think I can patch her up perfectly, and no one will know what she went through."

For a moment I thought he was talking about me, and I almost burst into tears. Not because I was hurt or offended by his words, but rather because the emotions I wear so close to the surface often bubble up from some place deep within me. It is in remembering my desire to be good but wild, loquacious but poised, energetic yet calm, that I finally realized my need to be seen for who I am. What I have been through is a revelation of identity—accepting myself and all my personality quirks, while also desiring to grow and evolve into a woman who is comfortable in her own skin. When Kevin innocently remarked on the work to be done on our beautiful wood floors, he reminded me of the delicate nature of change. It would require finesse and kindness with what already existed to make a change that would be lasting.

Now, every time I step off the bottom tread of our stairs and my foot rests on the intricate border of multiple wood species fitted together like a puzzle of warmth, I am grateful for trees planted and growing toward the sky. I can look out any window of our home, watching the breeze catch the upper branches of the oak, the Japanese maple, the magnolia, or the tall pine, and be reminded of my own internal growth. I bow in gratitude for changes in me that form their own visible circles where age is also measured internally, for workers who still care deeply about their craft, and for a very old house I call home.

Carriage House

All the sounds dear to a horseman were around me . . .
little sounds of no importance, but they stay in the
unconscious library of memory.
  —Wynford Vaughan-Thomas, *Madly in All Directions*

At the end of our driveway sits an old carriage house. It was converted to a garage for automobiles and things like bicycles, tools, and yard equipment a long time ago. It is here that I park my car each night while Andy's truck stays outside, unable to fit into the converted garage's shallow depth. In 1903, carriages were not as long as trucks. I suppose that, if measured, horse and carriage together would have a longer length than a Ford truck, but horses were unhitched from carriages and led to their stalls while the buggy would be wheeled into a separate room. When I walk into our converted garage, I can see exactly where the buggy would have been stored and where the horses bedded down for the night, each in their individual stall.

An overhead garage door, complete with an automatic opener, now replaces the old swing doors from the early 1900s, which would have been part of the original design of this space. Rather than press a button from a remote in my car to open the door and drive in, the buggy driver would have stepped down from his seat and walked to the front of the carriage house, opened the swing doors one by one, and then returned to unhitch the horses. This hitching and unhitching of the horses were part of a procedure that meant life was less complicated and urgent but seemingly more elegant. Rote tasks attached to the daily labors of the day provided a sense of balance and accomplishment. I mull this over as I drive into the garage at the end of a busy day, pleased by the fact that this space has found a new function.

Long ago, a carriage house was a sign of prestige as much as function. The ritual of preparing a horse and buggy for a drive in the country is easy to imagine here. There still lingers the faint smell of leather, hay, and hide when walking into our garage on a musty day. The connection I feel to this house originates, in part, from these horses from the past.

I won my first art contest when I was seven years old. At Churchill Grammar School in Glen Ellyn, Illinois, the second-grade class had been furiously drawing and painting for days. Miss Pastor, our teacher, chose what she felt were the best examples of youthful seven-year-old exuberance more than real talent, and she taped up these art contest submissions high on the wall. Opposite the art display were the windows of the classroom, which faced the parking lot. Our local art teacher, who taught at several schools in the area each week, arrived on this singular day, strode into the classroom, and pointed right at the painting I had done of a horse's head.

"I saw this from the parking lot as I drove in, and it is the winner."

I was called to come up to the front of the class to receive a blue ribbon, which I still have. It is taped to the front of the old, torn painting—never framed, and stored in a trunk in the attic. My submission was bold strokes of color in blue and red and yellow, which gave the appearance of op-art gone mad, but the vision of a horse could still be seen clearly.

This singular event changed me. I went from having an average fixation with horses, common to most little girls growing up in a mildly suburban area where glimpses of horses could be caught, to an obsessed youngster who pretended to be a horse at recess. I became the horse expert, though I'd never ridden one, and made friends purposefully with anyone who owned a horse. Pam Nelson, whose family moved into the area when I was in the third grade, became my inseparable friend. Eventually, I learned to ride on Honeyman, her brother's pony, while she rode her Shetland, Tina. My education in all things horse-related came from getting on, falling off, getting on again, falling off again, and mucking out stalls in between. This pattern of learning is representative of how I have learned most lessons in life. Go full speed, trip and fall, repeat.

When I was in the sixth grade, my parents took me to an auction to look at horses. We were there all day with my brothers and sisters in tow, but I knew they were there for me. I fell in love with one of the horses, and we came a pinch away from buying it. We had no barn, not enough land, and could never afford boarding, but my parents almost bought this horse. At the end of the day, my mom took me to the car—an enormous station wagon where the boys never sat anywhere but the "way back"—and, choking back tears, she told me they could not buy me the horse because our yard was not big enough. I cried when I went to bed that night, nursing the hurt of a longing unsatisfied.

Somehow, my mom found a neighbor with kittens, and she carried one to my bed. I put the kitten on the floor and told my mom that I did not want a kitten; I wanted a horse. My mom put the kitten back on my bed, and I held her in a choke hold all night while I cried into her fur. It took me months to realize that my parents could not afford to buy me a horse. We didn't speak of such things. We were expected to work hard and be good, and asking for something as outrageous as a horse was evidence of a selfishness I had not realized I possessed. My inability to see past my own desires left me ashamed, and the next day, as I carried the kitten into the kitchen, I hung onto my mother, not wanting her to leave my side. Without saying a word, she stroked my hair every so often in a knowing way, understanding that true growth comes internally, which is far more important than the pencil lines on the wall. Decades later, I still think of this moment in my childhood when I learned that love is formed and harvested even through disappointment.

Much the same way, love also applies to our experience of home and hearth, where discovering new functions for existing space is satisfying and fulfilling. I especially love it when I can incorporate some of the old with the new. Salvaging thick original tiles and blending the pieces into a new and expanded floor design breathes life into what will be a new space, but with more depth and character. Hidden inside of me, too, are elements from long ago that need to be refurbished and then pushed forward into the light of day. Things like self-doubt and insecurity pop up now and then, suddenly reminding me of the early days of my life, when I wanted to fit in but felt so very different. Walking to and from grammar school, picking milkweed pods and carefully opening them to reveal the seeds inside, I was contemplative and serious. If I blew on the seeds, where would the floss take them? Where would life take me?

My thoughts as a little girl were not fully formed as to the future, but I knew I desired a less bouncy landing when big emotions tossed me around. I wanted to gentle my soul but couldn't name this. I think that looking at a large and possibly scary horse, and considering that I could run my little girl hands on the neck of this glorious animal, knowing it could toss its head and swish its tail with energetic enthusiasm, formed a kindred connection I related to. I connected through the hope of a similar and future ability to contain my enthusiasm about life: calm by choice, and effervescent with joy rather than fear.

This garage, this carriage house, pleases me and reminds me that tasks require patience to do them well. Horses need calm hands to lead them into cold steel bits, and my soul needs the same touch as it heads into the unknown territory of quiet.

The back door opens, and my daughter and granddaughters come in. I go out back to take newspapers to the carriage house, and Summer toddles after me on firm little legs. She helps me open the door to the converted garage and fill a bin with newspapers. We go inside and make hot chocolate with tiny marshmallows floating on top. I teach her how to blow softly before taking a sip. Looking out the back window of our kitchen to the carriage house beyond, I begin to tell my granddaughters about art contests and horses and buggy rides. These stories of life lived by their grandmother a long time ago paint a picture of resilience and patience that connects the old with the young—values and virtue, courage and creativity—all elements of a life well lived and ready to be told fresh and new to young hearts and minds. I realize that some of the best treasures our old house brings are the memories it inspires in me, even when I lived somewhere else.

Kindly We Go

Remember there's no such thing as a small act of kindness. Every act creates a ripple with no logical end.
　　　　　　　　　　—Scott Adams, *Reframe Your Brain*

I used to be bothered by the fact that I walk around with myself every day. I wake up behind these eyes and peer out of them no matter what I do or where I go. I know what is on the inside, and sometimes I am exhausted by the chaos and constant struggle to keep things organized. The eternal series of corridors, passageways, and entrance and exit points in my mind's contents bogs me down, as I am easily distracted.

Often, I have crisply strode toward a piece of information in my mind, only to wander through my maze of thoughts, unable to retrieve what I am looking for. This information is necessary now, relevant to the conversation I am having, but as I enter my mental rooms I find the doorways interesting, and I wonder about the type of wood it would take to create a mantel for a project I am working on, and so I am distracted as I ruminate over this.

The conversation around me continues, and my face takes on a blank stare while I consider wood species. I started out looking to contribute to a conversation about the eighteenth-century Great Awakening in America, but the information I was looking for lurked behind a memory wall I couldn't penetrate, until I woke up in the middle of the night, sat up, and proclaimed, "Jonathan Edwards!" Andy wakes up and says, "Who?" and I say, "What?" and we sleep again.

Growing my inner self to keep pace with the aging and slowing down of my body had me reflecting on the subtle yet strategic changes that had taken place by transforming my environment. Moving away from a constant city electricity into a quieter world, where fields of corn expand beyond the horizon, surprised me at first and ultimately delighted me. I could enjoy the swish sound of tall grasses or a leisurely stroll around the town square without wanting to rush off to accomplish something. I began to see that being thorough didn't always have to mean fast.

Andy and I decided at the beginning of our old house remodel marathon that we would not do a slapdash job, putting quick fixes into the nightmares that would most certainly arise. We were both in line, emotionally, with slower repairs and reflective decisions when possible. This helped us create a more tranquil and less rushed mood while tackling each remodeling decision and necessity. The road had already been long, with many a tributary dart down an unknown path of discovery, but in staying the course, we now knew the core of our house, the beauty of her. In the relationship of trust we developed between house and home, we learned about ourselves. Andy was methodical in both his discoveries of what needed to be done and his ability to carefully coordinate each improvement, and I learned patience. Always one to believe that the right tool for the right job is the right way, he taught me to be precise and slow down. While growing in my listening capabilities, I leapt at every chance to do something new, exciting, and different, but I was able to give each idea a simmering period. Andy learned to give it a chance, to hear me out, to ponder and consider, even while watching me brandish my arms in wide sweeps as I explained the beauty of a new idea.

Core home improvements are hard-won victories, and internal core improvements of the soul are equally difficult. For each project brought to completion by hammer and nail, our souls were quieted as we grew together until we and the house became inseparable.

Balancing the ubiquitous ego that rises out of the ocean of self—sometimes as a monster but occasionally as something lovely—can be influenced, then tended. Andy and I began to see that our own ideas for this house were not originating only in us. We were learning how to listen to each other and to our abode. My lovely house had woven a common thread, a cord, a tether into my life. It haltered me and led me down healthier roads. It was taking me to the places of the mind where I needed to go. I needed kindness, and so I was kinder to myself.

I experienced kindness as a baby when my big brother Toddy filled my two-week-old mouth full of white sugar from a bowl in the kitchen. My sugary white lips and wide eyes were discovered by my mother moments later, and Toddy, standing with an empty bowl in his two-year-old hands, was evidence of him wanting to do something nice for his new baby sister. Of course, I have been told this story again and again, and I still smile as I think of my big brother "trining," as we would come to say.

It is one thing to experience kindness, and quite another to learn to dole it out ourselves. Working toward the value of kindness is like seeing a light far, far away and making progress toward that light to find that sinew and substance and strength stretch toward indescribable beauty. Reaching forward always, but with a gentleness that allows for the stretch without snapping in two—this was my eureka moment. Little by little, working toward one kind moment at a time, progress comes.

Kindness is not in the act. The most naïve among us know this. The tone of your life is not the act you do, but the manner and mood in which you do it. The dollar stuffed with a mutter and an oath into an outstretched hand breeds nothing if not resentment.

My mind needs to be exercised with kindness to allow me time away from self, where I can wander into other people's light and glow from the inside. All around me are those I love the most, and the radiance of their lives beckons me. I want to abide with them and not merely exist in my own world.

This old house has healed me by moving me into a land of simple truths that were planted inside me years ago—values learned from parents, siblings, grandparents. I am surrounded by a great cloud of witnesses.

The weeds of responsibility had a chokehold on me for a long time as I raised my family and ran a business. I treated each day as something to be accomplished rather than something to be experienced and enjoyed. But now, slowly, I have been pulling these weeds out of the ground and replacing them with soft boards, warm plaster, expansive windows of rippled glass, and meandering old brick pathways through the trees. In the process, I am learning to slow down and look with eyes of wonder at the kindness all around me.

Trees

Rest is not idleness, and to lie sometimes on the grass under trees on a summer's day, listening to the murmur of the water, or watching the clouds float across the sky, is by no means a waste of time.

—John Lubbock, *The Use of Life*

Looking out every window of our home, we see a tree peeking in to say hello. I smile, believing we are friends. In the city, trees are punctuation points on horizontal and vertical landscapes, tightly placed together, reminding us that there is a natural world to be enjoyed. Country trees do not pay attention to defined rules and meander their branches out and up into the open space beyond. My relationship with trees was born of a childhood surrounded by a variety of Midwestern foliage.

When I was a child, my mother and father often took us gaggle of kids to an arboretum, where I would walk with a branch in my hand, mimicking my mother. The stick meant we were walking in the woods, and this appendage seemed necessary, so my siblings and I searched for walking sticks first thing upon arrival.-

Running ahead of my parents, we would poke around, uncovering acorns or tracing pictures in the dirt with our sticks, aimless yet focused. It was here that we learned the words to most of the songs heard in musicals at the time— *The Sound of Music*, *Fiddler on the Roof*, and *The Music Man*. We shouted out the songs as we walked. *My Fair Lady* dazzled me, so I memorized and performed its songs in our living room for many years. The trees were pleasant audiences to our performances and gentle giants in the background of my earliest outdoor memories.

Elm trees loomed large and sprawling in the 1960s, just screaming to be climbed, before they all had to be cut down due to Dutch elm disease. It felt like death was upon us, but we took up residence in the maple trees all around us and soon forgot about the constant sound of chain saws in the background of our childhood tree-exploration years.

I loved the apple trees in the spring because of the flowering buds that were there one moment and gone the next. The apples seemed secondary to me, as I greeted the blossoms every year in other yards and then soon forgot them, fickle in my attention. One of my girlfriends in the neighborhood had the perfect climbing tree. Up we went, playing dolls in the branches, pretending we lived there permanently. Our playtime in the trees consisted of stories of abandonment or natural disaster. The tree was our home now.

Oak trees were special to me because of the multitude of them clustered at my namesake grandmother's home. Hunting for acorns passed the time while we waited for our parents to let us go swimming in her lake.

The cottonwood tree at our home in Wheaton was beautiful, except in the spring when the seedlings would blow their fluff everywhere, sticking to the screens of our windows, our hair, and our clothes. My father endured this tree, threatening to cut it down, even though its shade was lovely and appreciated.

As I walk the border of our country yard, I pass tall pine trees that sway softly in the breeze. Long needles drop to the ground and crunch underfoot where pinecones lay scattered haphazardly. Clyde picks one up in his mouth and runs wild for a moment before abandoning this toy for something else that grabs his attention. Dark green arborvitae line one side of the yard, forming a hedge and obscuring the neighboring view. I love the privacy this provides, though I can still peek through to see shapes, colors, and shadows. The patio is shadowed by a tall and beautiful poplar, where leaves bud late, but we wait and are always thrilled when they do.

Andy comes home from work each day, parking his truck beneath a walnut tree branching out over the driveway. Opening the back door, he sets his lunch box down and heads to the outdoor table that sits on old brick. There, he stares blankly toward the back of our yard while petting Clyde with large carpenter hands. I used to be jealous of the way he would arrive each day with a lovely routine that seemed impossible to achieve. Quiet contemplation, never hurried but accomplishing the unimaginable—Andy knows how to change gears with grace. I would never arrive home and take time to go and sit and frazzle the top of Clyde's head. I thought I didn't have time. I couldn't make time. I wouldn't make time. The fact that this is becoming the Old Testament of my behavior encourages me that more changes lie on the horizon. Simple decisions of quiet are made one moment at a time, eventually piling up enough to form a pattern. These new patterns light a glow of warmth within me. I am not done. I can change.

Today I arrived home from work after Andy and saw him sitting outside, so I parked my car under the walnut tree. I opened the back door to the house and set my bags down just inside, returning to sit in a chair on the old brick under the poplar tree and stare out toward the back. Clyde came over to me and sniffed around my open hand for the love he knew he would receive. Andy reached to pull my chair close to him, and I smiled at him, not speaking. We both returned our gazes to the various shapes of leaves swaying melodiously at the back of the yard.

This is better. Yes. This is a better way to come home.

Blinking

The bright sun . . . burst upon the crowded city in clear and radiant glory.

       —Charles Dickens, *Oliver Twist*

When I was five years old, I loved a book titled *Rowdy and Apron Strings*. The simple storyline had twin bear cubs emerging in the early spring from their dark cave into the splendor of sunlight. There was something about the hopefulness, the playfulness, the newness, and the adventure that captured my yet uncluttered heart. I read this book repeatedly, getting it out of our old library, even after I had moved on to more compelling and longer stories. Perhaps I could relate to the mischief, or maybe I felt a kinship with the dichotomy between Rowdy's independence and Apron Strings's neediness, but I think I connected, subliminally, to the idea of measuring joy within the manageable constraints of a single day.

Days are what we have. They begin and they end, and the in-between is where life happens. We have surely all experienced the promise of the clean slate, the bright and shining beginning, the past left behind, and the forward trajectory that a sunrise displays, all to eventually end with a slow dwindle, a snuffed-out spark of inspiration where only a sputtered memory remains. In contrast to the long and winding road of broken resolutions, a single day can bring a small but glorious piece of success into the otherwise disappointing space of unfulfilled promises and elusive goals.

I need a day to do something for me, bordering on compulsion. I am goal-oriented, to the imagined irritation of everyone around me. This includes an ever-patient husband and grown daughters who indulge their mother with her plans that must be accomplished now—jump in, no time, quick hurry, zip-zip, get it done. Why be patient when a headlong rush ahead will do? I am often embarrassed by my enthusiasm, since I imagine others viewing me with wide-eyed shock at my emotional displays.

In the past, when overwhelmed with introspection, I would have marched into a tunnel of self-reflection and sat on a rock, disappointed by my inability to relax and be calm in response to events happening around me. Our aging lady of a house, though, is helping me. She has given me just enough pause to see myself better, accept who I am, and move forward with the grace I see in her bones.

As I sip hot coffee, I look around and ponder our completed remodeling projects: warm wood floors underfoot and the gleam of polished plaster on the walls broadcasting a rich glow that makes me feel softer, gentler, more comfortable, and balanced. I see leaded glass, stained glass, and sand glass, so that looking outward to the world outside is satisfying—each window is unique and confident in its simplicity. I run my fingers up the banister as I head to the bedroom to get dressed, stopping to open the little doors in the second-floor foyer. I stare at the wall covering of animals climbing trees lining these little alcoves and smile to think of how this delights me. I select my outfit for this day and dress carefully, thinking about each task in front of me, each interaction I will have, the privilege of human contact. I do not want to miss a thing, so I take my time. I sit for a moment and let the day's agenda soak into me.

I marvel at how much can be done in a single day. We measure our accomplishments in days: organizing closets (2.5 days), time between hair highlights (56 days), gaining weight around the middle (.005 day), births (280 days), a long life (32,850 days), potty training (497 days), and loving a child (infinite days). But what is unique to life daily is the moment-to-moment experience of time between sunrise and sunset. The day dawns before us, and we fill it—with the mundane and the extraordinary.

As a child, days loomed long, filled with food and fun and friends and siblings and stories and chores and homework—and "help your mother," "play nice," and "work hard." The waiting in between, for the days at a cabin in the woods or on a beach, seemed eternal. Now, a day is five minutes, a week is eight hours, a month is three days, and a year passes if I turn my head for a moment.

So, what to do with this day? The options are limitless and not limited to tasks. My today is what my mind says it is. Tasks are reactions, in a way. I am good at this. I can assess when some physical thing needs to be done and make it so. My education of late, though, has been to see the things I am not good at. I am learning to see the world from a nontask viewpoint. The hard ground of my soul has needed to be tilled and softened to see wonder and patience and peace and pondering. This house has taught me that. It waited patiently for our loving hands to smooth its craggy surfaces, and together we have breathed a sigh of relief.

I have learned that I am responsible for my reactions to the hum of life around me. The core of Maida hasn't changed, but my ability to see past myself has expanded. I have found a new and gentler land, filled with infinite possibility. I am happy, and so I listen to Mario Lanza sing "Be My Love." I sing loudly with abandon, accompanying his perfect tenor with my off-key middle of the road. I start laundry, make a grocery list, prepare for a client meeting, sketch out a new floor plan for a project, mull over my hair, walk five miles, answer my daughter's texts, make plans to drive to a little café where we can sit outside, cry with a friend, call Andy to hear his voice, and be inspired by the book I hold in my hand. It is now late afternoon, and I can make the rest of today anything I want it to be—no matter what comes, no matter the barrage of information pouring at me out of a firehose, I get to decide my soul's response as I walk, blinking, into the sunlight that is today.

Acknowledgments

I have so many to thank, because I can rarely do anything of substance without my great cloud of witnesses. Kimberly, Kerianne, Heather, and Miranda—you are my muses, my great loves, and the ones who tell me the truth no matter what. My parents, for the books that filled the walls of my childhood, and my siblings, who have never stopped being the people I want to talk to the most. I love you all beyond measure. Jenny, you know who you are to me, but I'll keep telling you. Maria S., you are in much of my writing because we met when we were young and thought we were wise. Hah! Karen and Ingrid, friends forever who never stopped encouraging me. Kathy E., and Maria C., your love and wise counsel have been cornerstones. And Deb L., your belief in my writing has been a guiding light.

Brooke Warner, thank you for all your guidance and expertise, and just wow. What an example of hurricane meets calm. You inspire me. And to Megan Milton, Kathleen Furin, Anne Durette, and all my SWP sisters, I am so grateful for you and would be lost without your expertise. Suzie, my first reader, your input was unwavering and indispensable. Alan, never stop saying, 'But why?' And without the gems from Marion, I would not have shiny objects before me. Jane Brox, Kyoko Mori, Pamela Petro—my first mentors—I owe you a debt of thanks. Huge thanks also to my cover designers, interior page layout and design teams, editors, and all those whose knowledge of such things extends far, far beyond mine.

Everyone at She Writes Press and Simon & Schuster, I bow to you in gratitude. This mewling is growing because of you and your superhuman level of care. To my marketing team at Mindbuck Media Group, an enormous round of thanks.

To my readers, you are whom I think about when I spread open my fingers and place them on the keys. For you, I go to the chair.

And to Andy, my sounding board and the platform on which I stand. My boot-stomping man. I love you.

About the Author

Maida Korte loves to write about the intersection of interior design and family life, revealing the humor, heart, and lessons found in both. A Midwestern native with a tireless work ethic, she raised four daughters while running a design firm—an experience she jokes qualifies her to run a small country.

A former HGTV guest, she holds a Bachelor of Science in Interior Design and a Master of Fine Arts in Creative Writing. She has won multiple awards for her design work and was recently short-listed by *The Letter Review* for her essays. *Gutted: How an Old House Remodeled Me* is her debut book.

Maida lives at the intersection of family, faith, and frivolity, and resides in Lake in the Hills, Illinois, with her husband.

Learn more about her work at www.maidakorte.com or subscribe to her newsletter at www.maidakorte.substack.com.

Author photo © Lydia Esther Photography

Looking for your next great read?

We can help!

Visit www.shewritespress.com/next-read
or scan the QR code below for a list
of our recommended titles.

She Writes Press is an award-winning
independent publishing company founded to
serve women writers everywhere.